What's in a name? That which we call a rose
By any other word would smell as sweet.

The Tragedy of Romeo and Juliet

Act II, Scene 2

THE TRAGEDY OF ROMEO AND JULIET

William Shakespeare

with Connections

209

HOLT, RINEHART AND WINSTON
Harcourt Brace & Company

Austin • New York • Orlando • Atlanta • San Francisco
Boston • Dallas • Toronto • London

For permission to reprint copyrighted material, grateful acknowledgment is made to the following sources:

The New York Times Company: From "In America; Romeo and Juliet in Bosnia" by Bob Herbert from *The New York Times,* May 8, 1994. Copyright © 1994 by The New York Times Company.
The Wall Street Journal: From "Juliet of Verona Gets a Lot of Letters from the Lovelorn" by Lisa Bannon from *The Wall Street Journal,* November 10, 1992. Copyright © 1992 by Dow Jones & Company, Inc. All rights reserved worldwide.

Cover art: Joe Melomo, Design Director; Shoehorn, Inc., Designer; Andrew Yates, Photographer; Mike Gobbi, Photo Researcher

ISBN 0-03-057304-1   10 11 043 06 05

CONTENTS

William Shakespeare
(1564–1616)

He is the most famous writer in the world, but he left us no journals or letters—he left us only his poems and his plays. What we know about William Shakespeare's personal life comes mostly from church and legal documents—a baptismal registration, a marriage license, and records of real-estate transactions. We also have a few remarks that others wrote about him during his lifetime.

We know that William was born the third of eight children, around April 23, 1564, in Stratford, a market town about one hundred miles northwest of London. His father, John, was a shopkeeper and a man of some importance in Stratford, serving at various times as justice of the peace and high bailiff (mayor).

William attended grammar school, where he studied Latin grammar, Latin literature, and rhetoric (the uses of language). As far as we know, he had no further formal education.

At the age of eighteen, he married Anne Hathaway, who was eight years older than he was. Some time after the birth of their second and third children (twins), Shakespeare moved to London, apparently leaving his family in Stratford.

We know that several years later, by 1592, Shakespeare had already become an actor and a playwright. By 1594, he was a charter member of the theatrical company called the Lord Chamberlain's Men, which was later to become the King's Men. (As the names of these acting companies indicate, theatrical groups depended on the support of a wealthy patron—the King's Men were supported by King James himself.) Shakespeare worked with this company for the rest of his writing life. Year after year, he provided it with plays, almost on demand. Shakespeare was the ultimate professional writer. He had a theater that needed plays, actors who needed parts, and a family that needed to be fed.

Romeo and Juliet was probably among the early plays that Shakespeare wrote between 1594 and 1596. By 1612, when he returned to Stratford to live the life of a prosperous retired gentleman, Shakespeare had written thirty-seven plays, including such masterpieces as *Julius Caesar, Hamlet, Othello, King Lear,* and *Macbeth.*

Shakespeare's plays are still produced all over the world. During a Broadway season in the 1980s, one critic estimated that if Shakespeare were alive, he would be receiving $25,000 a week in royalties for a production of *Othello* alone. The play was attracting larger audiences than any other nonmusical production in town.

Shakespeare died on April 23, 1616, at the age of fifty-two. He is buried under the old stone floor in the chancel of Holy Trinity church in Stratford. Carved over his grave is the following verse (the spelling is modernized):

Good friend, for Jesus' sake forbear
To dig the dust enclosed here.
Blessed be the man that spares these stones
And cursed be he that moves my bones.

These are hardly the best of Shakespeare's lines (if indeed they are his at all), but like his other lines, they seem to have worked. His bones lie undisturbed to this day.

Shakespeare and His Theater: A Perfect Match

Sometimes playwrights influence the shape and form of a theater, but more often existing theaters seem to influence the shape and form of plays. It is important that we understand Shakespeare's theater because it influenced how he wrote his plays. Shakespeare took the theater of his time, and he used it brilliantly.

The "Wooden O"

In 1576, outside the city walls of London, an actor-manager named James Burbage built the first permanent theater in England. He called it The Theater. Up to that time, touring acting companies had played wherever they could rent space. Usually this would be in the courtyards of inns. There the actors would erect a temporary platform stage at one end of the yard and play to an audience that stood around the stage or sat in the tiers of balconies that surrounded the courtyard. (Normally these balconies were used as passageways to the various rooms of the inn.) It was natural, then, that the first theater built by Burbage should derive its shape and form from the inns.

In 1599, Burbage's theater was torn down, and its timbers were used by Shakespeare and his company to build the Globe Theater. This was the theater for which Shakespeare wrote most of his plays.

In his play *Henry V,* Shakespeare called his theater a "wooden O." It was a large, round (or polygonal) building, three stories high, with a large platform stage that projected from one end into a yard open to the sky. In the back wall of this stage was a curtained-off inner stage. Flanking the inner stage were two doors for entrances and exits. Above this inner stage was a small balcony or upper stage, which could be used to suggest Juliet's balcony or the high walls of a castle or the bridge of a ship. Trapdoors were placed in the floor of the main stage for the entrances and exits of ghosts and for descents into hell.

The plays were performed in the afternoon. Since the stage was open to the sky, there was no need for stage illumination. There were very few sets (scenery, furniture, etc.). The stage was "set" by the language. A whole forest scene is created in one play when a character announces: "Well, this is the Forest of Arden." But costumes were often elaborate, and the stage might be hung with colorful banners and trappings. (The groundlings, those eight hundred or more people who stood shoulder to shoulder around the stage for the price of a penny, loved a good show. Most people still do.)

We can see that this stage, with its few sets and many acting areas—forestage, inner stage, and upper stage—made for a theater of great fluidity. That is, scene could follow scene with almost cinematic ease.

In one interesting aspect, the theater in Shakespeare's day was very different from the theater we know today. Acting wasn't considered entirely respectable by the English Puritans, so all women's parts were played by boys. Not for many years did women appear onstage in the professional English theater. In Shakespeare's day, Juliet would have been played by a trained boy actor.

The Modern Stage: Back to Shakespeare's Theater

It has been said that all you need for a theater is "two planks and a passion." Since Shakespeare's time "the planks" (the stage) have undergone various changes. First, the part of the stage which projected into the yard grew narrower, and the small curtained inner stage grew larger, until there developed what is called the **proscenium stage**. Here, there is no outer stage; there is only the inner stage, and a large curtain separates it from the audience. The effect is like looking inside a window or inside a picture frame. This is the stage most of us know today. It has been standard for well over a hundred years.

But recently, we have seen a reversal of this design. Now, more and more theaters (especially university and regional theaters) are building "thrust" stages, or arena stages. In this kind of theater, the audience once again sits on three or even four sides of the stage.

The Movies and the Theater: Words vs. Action
Like Shakespeare's stage, this kind of "thrust" stage, with its minimal scenery, allows playwrights (if they want) to move their stories rapidly from place to place. They can establish each new scene with a line like "Well, this is the Forest of Arden." As a result, playwrights have been tempted to write plays that imitate the style of movies. But this imitation rarely works. Theater and movies are two different media. A theater audience does not necessarily want to be whisked from place to place. People who go to plays often prefer to spend a long, long time watching the subtle development of conflicts among a small group of people, all in one setting. For example, all of the action in Lorraine Hansberry's play *A Raisin in the Sun* takes place inside one small apartment on Chicago's South Side.

Movies are basically a *visual* medium and so must chiefly engage and delight the eye, rather than the ear. (One movie director once referred to a dialogue in a movie as "foreground *noise*"!) The theater is much more a medium of *words*. When we go to see a play, it is the movement of the *words* rather than the movement of the scenery that delights us.

This difference between the appeal of a movie and the appeal of a play may account for the failure of some successful plays when they are translated to the screen. The movie producer will say: "Open up the story." In "opening up the story," the producer sometimes loses the concentration, the intensity, which was the prime virtue of the play.

Background on the Play

Romeo and Juliet, a very young man and a nearly fourteen-year-old girl, fall in love at first sight. They are caught up in an idealized, almost unreal, passionate love. They are in love with love. In his Prologue, Brooke preaches a moral, which people of his time expected. He says that Romeo and Juliet had to die because they broke the laws and married unwisely, against their parents' wishes. But Shakespeare does away with this moralizing. He presents the couple as "star-crossed lovers," doomed to disaster by fate.

To understand what *star-crossed* means, you have to realize that most people of Shakespeare's time believed in astrology. They believed that the course of their lives was partly determined by the hour, day, month, and year of their birth—hence, "the star" under which they were born. But Shakespeare may not have shared this belief. In a later play, *Julius Caesar*, Shakespeare has a character question this old idea about astrology and the influence of the stars:

> The fault, dear Brutus, is not in our stars,
> But in ourselves that we are underlings.

Although Shakespeare says in the Prologue that Romeo and Juliet are star-crossed, he does not make them mere victims of fate. Romeo and Juliet make decisions that lead to their disaster. More important, other characters have a hand in the play's tragic ending. How important do *you* think fate is in affecting what happens to us? To what degree do you think we control our own destinies?

How to Read Shakespeare

A Word List

Shakespeare wrote this play about four hundred years ago. It's not surprising, then, that many words are by now **archaic,** which means that they (or their particular meanings) have fallen out of common use. The footnotes in the play will help you with these archaic words and with other words and expressions that might be unfamiliar to you. Here are some of the archaic words that are repeatedly used in the play.

'a: he.
a': on.
an' or **and:** if.
Anon!: Soon! Right away! Coming!
but: if, or only.
Good-den or **go-den** or **God-den:** Good evening.
  (This was said in the late afternoon.)
hap or **happy:** luck, or lucky.
humor: mood, or moisture.
Jack: common fellow, ordinary guy.
maid: unmarried girl.
mark: listen to.
Marry!: mild oath, shortened from "By the Virgin
  Mary!"
nice: trivial, foolish.
owes: owns.
shrift: confession or forgiveness for sins that have
  been confessed to a priest. After confession a
  person was said to be **shriven.**

Soft!: Quiet! Hush! Slow up!
Stay!: Wait!
withal: with that, with.
wot: know.

The Poetry

Whatever Shakespeare learned of rhetoric, or language, in grammar school, he parades with relish in *Romeo and Juliet*. He is obviously having a fine time here with puns and word-play and all the other variations he can ring on the English language.

Romeo and Juliet is written in both prose and poetry. Prose is for the most part spoken by the common people and occasionally by Mercutio when he is joking. Most of the other characters speak in poetry.

Blank verse. The poetry is largely written in unrhymed iambic pentameter. In **iambic meter** each unstressed syllable is followed by a stressed syllable, as in the word *prefér*. In **iambic pentameter** there are five of these iambic units in each line. Unrhymed iambic pentameter is called **blank verse.** The word *blank* just means that there is no rhyme at the end of lines.

Read aloud this perfect example of iambic pentameter, spoken by Romeo. The syllables marked (') should be stressed.

But soft! What light through yonder window breaks?

Couplets. When Shakespeare uses rhymes, he generally uses **couplets,** two consecutive lines of poetry that rhyme. The couplets often punctuate a character's exit or signal the end of a scene. Read aloud Juliet's exit line from the balcony.

Good night, good night! Parting is such sweet sorrow
That I shall say good night till it be morrow.

Reading the lines. We have all heard people ruin a good poem by mechanically pausing at the end of each line, whether or not the meaning of the line called for such a pause. (Maxwell Anderson, who wrote verse plays, had his plays typed as though they were prose, so that actors would not be tempted to pause at the end of each line. Directors of Shakespeare's plays today often advise actors to do the same.)

Lines of poetry are either end-stopped lines or run-on lines. An **end-stopped line** has some punctuation at its end. A **run-on line** has no punctuation at its end. In a run-on line, the meaning is completed in the line or lines that follow.

Try reading aloud this passage from Act II, Scene 2, where Juliet speaks in end-stopped lines—lines ending with punctuation that requires her to pause:

> O, Romeo, Romeo! Wherefore art thou Romeo?
> Deny thy father and refuse thy name;
> Or, if thou wilt not, be but sworn my love,
> And I'll no longer be a Capulet.

But Romeo's speech in the same scene has many run-on lines. Read these lines aloud; where does Romeo pause?

> The brightness of her cheek would shame those stars
> As daylight doth a lamp; her eyes in heaven
> Would through the airy region stream so bright
> That birds would sing and think it were not night.

The glory of *Romeo and Juliet* is its poetry and its theatricality. The play is fast moving, and the poetry suits the story of young people dealing with a matter very important to them—passionate, once-in-a-lifetime love.

The Tragedy of Romeo and Juliet

by
William Shakespeare

Characters

The Montagues
LORD MONTAGUE
LADY MONTAGUE
ROMEO, son of Montague
BENVOLIO, nephew of Montague and friend of Romeo
BALTHASAR, servant of Romeo
ABRAM, servant of Montague

The Capulets
LORD CAPULET
LADY CAPULET
JULIET, daughter of Capulet
TYBALT, nephew of Lady Capulet
NURSE to Juliet
PETER, servant to the Nurse
SAMPSON ⎫
⎬ servants of Capulet
GREGORY ⎭
AN OLD MAN of the Capulet family

The Others
PRINCE ESCALUS, ruler of Verona
MERCUTIO, a relative of the Prince and friend of Romeo
FRIAR LAURENCE, a Franciscan priest
FRIAR JOHN, another Franciscan priest
COUNT PARIS, a young nobleman, a relative of the Prince
AN APOTHECARY (a druggist)
PAGE to Paris
CHIEF WATCHMAN
THREE MUSICIANS
AN OFFICER
CITIZENS OF VERONA, RELATIVES of both families, MASKERS,
GUARDS, WATCHMEN, and ATTENDANTS

Scene: Verona and Mantua, cities in northern Italy

The Prologue

Enter CHORUS.

Chorus.
Two households, both alike in dignity,°
    In fair Verona, where we lay our scene,
From ancient grudge break to new mutiny,
    Where civil blood makes civil hands unclean.°
From forth the fatal loins of these two foes   5
    A pair of star-crossed lovers take their life;
Whose misadventured piteous overthrows
    Do with their death bury their parents' strife.
The fearful passage of their death-marked love,
    And the continuance of their parents' rage,   10
Which, but° their children's end, naught could remove,
    Is now the two hours' traffic° of our stage;
The which if you with patient ears attend,
What here shall miss, our toil shall strive to mend.

Exit.

Pro.1. **dignity:** status.
   4.   That is, where civilians' passions ("civil blood") make their hands
        unclean (because they have been used for killing).
 11.   **but:** except for.
 12.   **traffic:** business.

Act I

Scene 1. *Verona. A public place.*

Enter SAMPSON *and* GREGORY, *of the house of Capulet, with swords and bucklers (shields).*

Sampson. Gregory, on my word, we'll not carry coals.°
Gregory. No, for then we should be colliers.°
Sampson. I mean, and° we be in choler,° we'll draw.°
Gregory. Ay, while you live, draw your neck out of
    collar.°   5
Sampson. I strike quickly, being moved.
Gregory. But thou art not quickly moved to strike.
Sampson. A dog of the house of Montague moves me.
Gregory. To move is to stir, and to be valiant is to stand.
    Therefore, if thou art moved, thou run'st away.   10
Sampson. A dog of that house shall move me to stand. I
    will take the wall° of any man or maid of Montague's.
Gregory. That shows thee a weak slave; for the weakest
    goes to the wall.°
Sampson. 'Tis true; and therefore women, being the   15
    weaker vessels, are ever thrust to the wall. Therefore
    I will push Montague's men from the wall and
    thrust his maids to the wall.

I.1.1.   **carry coals:** do dirty work (put up with insults). People often made
    jokes about men who carted coal.
  2.   **colliers:** coal dealers (men with dirty jobs). Notice how the servants
    start making jokes based on words that sound similar (*colliers, choler,*
    and *collar*).
  3.   **and:** if. **choler:** anger. **draw:** pull out swords.
  5.   **collar:** the hangman's noose.
  12.   **take the wall:** take the best place on the path (which is closest to the wall).
  14.   **goes to the wall:** is defeated.

Gregory. The quarrel is between our masters and us
their men.   20
Sampson. 'Tis all one. I will show myself a tyrant.
When I have fought with the men, I will be civil
with the maids—I will cut off their heads.
Gregory. The heads of the maids?
Sampson. Ay, the heads of the maids or their maiden-   25
heads. Take it in what sense thou wilt.
Gregory. They must take it in sense that feel it.
Sampson. Me they shall feel while I am able to stand;
and 'tis known I am a pretty piece of flesh.
Gregory. 'Tis well thou art not fish; if thou hadst, thou   30
hadst been Poor John.° Draw thy tool!° Here comes
two of the house of Montagues.

Enter two other servingmen, ABRAM *and* BALTHASAR.

Sampson. My naked weapon is out. Quarrel! I will
back thee.
Gregory. How? Turn thy back and run?   35
Sampson. Fear me not.°
Gregory. No, marry. I fear thee!
Sampson. Let us take the law of our sides;° let them
begin.
Gregory. I will frown as I pass by, and let them take it as   40
they list.
Sampson. Nay, as they dare. I will bite my thumb° at
them, which is disgrace to them if they bear it.
Abram. Do you bite your thumb at us, sir?
Sampson. I do bite my thumb, sir.   45
Abram. Do you bite your thumb at us, sir?
Sampson [*aside to* GREGORY]. Is the law of our side if I
say ay?

---

31. **Poor John:** kind of salted fish, a poor person's food. **tool:** sword.
36. **Fear me not:** Do not distrust me.
38. That is, stay on the right side of the law.
42. **bite my thumb:** an insulting gesture.

Gregory [*aside to* SAMPSON]. No.
Sampson. No, sir, I do not bite my thumb at you, sir; but   50
    I bite my thumb, sir.
Gregory. Do you quarrel, sir?
Abram. Quarrel, sir? No, sir.
Sampson. But if you do, sir, I am for you. I serve as good
    a man as you.   55
Abram. No better.
Sampson. Well, sir.

Enter BENVOLIO.

Gregory. Say "better." Here comes one of my master's
    kinsmen.
Sampson. Yes, better, sir.   60
Abram. You lie.
Sampson. Draw, if you be men. Gregory, remember thy
    swashing° blow.

They fight.

Benvolio.
    Part, fools!
    Put up your swords. You know not what you do.   65

Enter TYBALT.

Tybalt.
    What, art thou drawn among these heartless hinds?°
    Turn thee, Benvolio; look upon thy death.
Benvolio.
    I do but keep the peace. Put up thy sword,
    Or manage it to part these men with me.
Tybalt.
    What, drawn, and talk of peace? I hate the word   70
    As I hate hell, all Montagues, and thee.
    Have at thee, coward!

---

63. **swashing:** smashing.
66. **heartless hinds:** cowardly hicks.

They fight.

Enter an OFFICER, *and three or four* CITIZENS *with clubs, bills, and partisans, or spears.*

Officer. Clubs, bills, and partisans! Strike! Beat them
down! Down with the Capulets! Down with the
Montagues! 75

Enter old CAPULET *in his gown, and his wife,* LADY CAPULET.

Capulet.
What noise is this? Give me my long sword, ho!
Lady Capulet.
A crutch, a crutch! Why call you for a sword?
Capulet.
My sword, I say! Old Montague is come
And flourishes his blade in spite of° me.

Enter old MONTAGUE *and his wife,* LADY MONTAGUE.

Montague.
Thou villain Capulet!—Hold me not; let me go. 80
Lady Montague.
Thou shalt not stir one foot to seek a foe.

Enter PRINCE ESCALUS, *with his* TRAIN.

Prince.
Rebellious subjects, enemies to peace,
Profaners of this neighbor-stainèd steel—
Will they not hear? What, ho! You men, you beasts,
That quench the fire of your pernicious rage 85
With purple fountains issuing from your veins!
On pain of torture, from those bloody hands
Throw your mistempered° weapons to the ground
And hear the sentence of your movèd prince.
Three civil brawls, bred of an airy° word 90

---

79. in spite of: in defiance of.
88. mistempered: used with bad temper.
90. airy: light.

By thee, old Capulet, and Montague,
Have thrice disturbed the quiet of our streets
And made Verona's ancient citizens
Cast by their grave beseeming° ornaments
To wield old partisans, in hands as old,   95
Cankered with peace, to part your cankered° hate.
If ever you disturb our streets again,
Your lives shall pay the forfeit of the peace.
For this time all the rest depart away.
You, Capulet, shall go along with me;   100
And, Montague, come you this afternoon,
To know our farther pleasure in this case,
To old Freetown, our common judgment place.
Once more, on pain of death, all men depart.

Exeunt all but MONTAGUE, LADY MONTAGUE, *and* BENVOLIO.

Montague.
Who set this ancient quarrel new abroach?°   105
Speak, nephew, were you by when it began?
Benvolio.
Here were the servants of your adversary
And yours, close fighting ere I did approach.
I drew to part them. In the instant came
The fiery Tybalt, with his sword prepared,   110
Which, as he breathed defiance to my ears,
He swung about his head and cut the winds,
Who, nothing hurt withal, hissed him in scorn.
While we were interchanging thrusts and blows,
Came more and more, and fought on part and part,°   115
Till the prince came, who parted either part.

---

94. **grave beseeming:** dignified, as they should be.
96. **cankered:** The first "cankered" means "rusted" (from lack of use in peaceful times); the second means "diseased," like a canker, a running sore.
105. **new abroach:** opened again.
115. **on part and part:** some on each side.

Lady Montague.
> O, where is Romeo? Saw you him today?
> Right glad I am he was not at this fray.

Benvolio.
> Madam, an hour before the worshiped sun
> Peered forth the golden window of the East,   120
> A troubled mind drave me to walk abroad;
> Where, underneath the grove of sycamore
> That westward rooteth from this city side,
> So early walking did I see your son.
> Towards him I made, but he was ware° of me   125
> And stole into the covert of the wood.
> I, measuring his affections by my own,
> Which then most sought where most might not be
>   found,°
> Being one too many by my weary self,
> Pursued my humor not pursuing his,   130
> And gladly shunned who gladly fled from me.

Montague.
> Many a morning hath he there been seen,
> With tears augmenting the fresh morning's dew,
> Adding to clouds more clouds with his deep sighs;
> But all so soon as the all-cheering sun   135
> Should in the farthest East begin to draw
> The shady curtains from Aurora's° bed,
> Away from light steals home my heavy° son
> And private in his chamber pens himself,
> Shuts up his windows, locks fair daylight out,   140
> And makes himself an artificial night.
> Black and portentous must this humor prove
> Unless good counsel may the cause remove.

---

125. ware: aware.
128. He sought a place where no one could be found. (He wanted to be
       alone.)
137. Aurora is goddess of the dawn.
138. heavy: heavy-hearted.

Benvolio.
My noble uncle, do you know the cause?
Montague.
I neither know it nor can learn of him.   145
Benvolio.
Have you importuned° him by any means?
Montague.
Both by myself and many other friends;
But he, his own affections' counselor,
Is to himself—I will not say how true—
But to himself so secret and so close,   150
So far from sounding° and discovery,
As is the bud bit with an envious° worm
Ere he can spread his sweet leaves to the air
Or dedicate his beauty to the sun.
Could we but learn from whence his sorrows grow,   155
We would as willingly give cure as know.

Enter ROMEO.

Benvolio.
See, where he comes. So please you step aside;
I'll know his grievance, or be much denied.
Montague.
I would thou wert so happy° by the stay
To hear true shrift.° Come, madam, let's away.   160

Exeunt MONTAGUE *and* LADY MONTAGUE.

Benvolio.
Good morrow, cousin.
Romeo.   Is the day so young?

---

146. **importuned:** questioned.
151. **So far from sounding:** so far from being sounded out for his mood
      (as a river is sounded for its depth).
152. **envious:** evil.
159. **happy:** fortunate.
160. **shrift:** confession.

Benvolio.
But new struck nine.
Romeo.   Ay me! Sad hours seem long.
Was that my father that went hence so fast?
Benvolio.
It was. What sadness lengthens Romeo's hours?
Romeo.
Not having that which having makes them short.   165
Benvolio. In love?
Romeo. Out——
Benvolio. Of love?
Romeo.
Out of her favor where I am in love.
Benvolio.
Alas that love, so gentle in his view,°   170
Should be so tyrannous and rough in proof!°
Romeo.
Alas that love, whose view is muffled still,°
Should without eyes see pathways to his will!
Where shall we dine? O me! What fray was here?
Yet tell me not, for I have heard it all.   175
Here's much to do with hate, but more with love.°
Why then, O brawling love, O loving hate,
O anything, of nothing first created!
O heavy lightness, serious vanity,
Misshapen chaos of well-seeming forms,   180
Feather of lead, bright smoke, cold fire, sick health,
Still-waking sleep, that is not what it is!
This love feel I, that feel no love in this.
Dost thou not laugh?
Benvolio.   No, coz,° I rather weep.

---

170. **view:** appearance.
171. **in proof:** in reality.
172. **muffled still:** always blindfolded. Romeo is talking about Cupid, who was depicted as blindfolded.
176. **more with love:** They like fighting.
184. **coz:** cousin (or other relative).

Romeo.
Good heart, at what?
Benvolio.   At thy good heart's oppression.   185
Romeo.
Why, such is love's transgression.
Griefs of mine own lie heavy in my breast,
Which thou wilt propagate,° to have it prest°
With more of thine. This love that thou hast shown
Doth add more grief to too much of mine own.   190
Love is a smoke made with the fume of sighs;
Being purged, a fire sparkling in lovers' eyes;
Being vexed, a sea nourished with loving tears.
What is it else? A madness most discreet,°
A choking gall, and a preserving sweet.   195
Farewell, my coz.
Benvolio.   Soft!° I will go along.
And if you leave me so, you do me wrong.
Romeo.
Tut! I have lost myself; I am not here;
This is not Romeo, he's some other where.
Benvolio.
Tell me in sadness,° who is that you love?   200
Romeo.
What, shall I groan and tell thee?
Benvolio.   Groan? Why, no;
But sadly tell me who.
Romeo.
Bid a sick man in sadness make his will.
Ah, word ill urged to one that is so ill!
In sadness, cousin, I do love a woman.   205
Benvolio.
I aimed so near when I supposed you loved.

---

188. **propagate:** increase. **prest:** burdened.
194. **discreet:** discriminating.
196. **Soft!:** Wait!
200. **sadness:** seriousness.

Romeo.
A right good markman. And she's fair I love.
Benvolio.
A right fair mark, fair coz, is soonest hit.
Romeo.
Well, in that hit you miss. She'll not be hit
With Cupid's arrow. She hath Dian's wit,° 210
And, in strong proof° of chastity well armed,
From Love's weak childish bow she lives uncharmed.
She will not stay° the siege of loving terms,
Nor bide th' encounter of assailing eyes,
Nor ope her lap to saint-seducing gold.° 215
O, she is rich in beauty; only poor
That, when she dies, with beauty dies her store.°
Benvolio.
Then she hath sworn that she will still live chaste?
Romeo.
She hath, and in that sparing makes huge waste;
For beauty, starved with her severity, 220
Cuts beauty off from all posterity.
She is too fair, too wise, wisely too fair,
To merit bliss° by making me despair.
She hath forsworn to love, and in that vow
Do I live dead that live to tell it now. 225
Benvolio.
Be ruled by me; forget to think of her.
Romeo.
O, teach me how I should forget to think!

---

210. **Dian's wit:** the cunning of Diana, the goddess of chastity, who was
not interested in men.
211. **proof:** armor.
213. **stay:** obey.
215. **Nor ope . . . gold:** In myth, the god Zeus visited Danae in the form of
a shower of gold, and Danae bore Zeus a son.
217. **when she dies . . . her store:** Her store of beauty dies with her, since
she'll have no children.
223. **bliss:** heaven.

Benvolio.
By giving liberty unto thine eyes.
Examine other beauties.
Romeo.   'Tis the way
To call hers, exquisite, in question° more.   230
These happy masks° that kiss fair ladies' brows,
Being black, put us in mind they hide the fair.
He that is strucken blind cannot forget
The precious treasure of his eyesight lost.
Show me a mistress that is passing fair: 235
What doth her beauty serve but as a note
Where I may read who passed that passing fair?
Farewell. Thou canst not teach me to forget.
Benvolio.
I'll pay that doctrine, or else die in debt.°

Exeunt.

Scene 2. *A street.*

Enter CAPULET, COUNT PARIS, *and the clown, his* SERVANT.

Capulet.
But Montague is bound° as well as I,
In penalty alike; and 'tis not hard, I think,
For men so old as we to keep the peace.
Paris.
Of honorable reckoning° are you both,
And pity 'tis you lived at odds so long.   5
But now, my lord, what say you to my suit?

---

230. **call . . . in question:** remind one of her beauty.
231. **masks:** Women often wore masks to protect their faces from the sun.
239. **or else die in debt:** or die trying.
I.2.1. **is bound:** is pledged to keep the peace.
   4. **reckoning:** reputation.

Capulet.
But saying o'er what I have said before:
My child is yet a stranger in the world,
She hath not seen the change of fourteen years;
Let two more summers wither in their pride   10
Ere we may think her ripe to be a bride.
Paris.
Younger than she are happy mothers made.
Capulet.
And too soon marred are those so early made.
Earth hath swallowed all my hopes but she;
She is the hopeful lady of my earth.   15
But woo her, gentle Paris, get her heart;
My will to her consent is but a part.
And she agreed, within her scope of choice°
Lies my consent and fair according° voice.
This night I hold an old accustomed° feast,   20
Whereto I have invited many a guest,
Such as I love; and you among the store,
One more, most welcome, makes my number more.
At my poor house look to behold this night
Earth-treading stars° that make dark heaven light. 25
Such comfort as do lusty young men feel
When well-appareled April on the heel
Of limping winter treads, even such delight
Among fresh fennel° buds shall you this night
Inherit° at my house. Hear all, all see,   30
And like her most whose merit most shall be;
Which, on more view of many, mine, being one,
May stand in number,° though in reck'ning none.°
Come, go with me.

---

18. **within her scope of choice:** among all she can choose from.
19. **according:** agreeing.
20. **accustomed:** traditional.
25. **Earth-treading stars:** that is, young girls.
29. **fennel:** an herb. Capulet compares the young girls to fennel flowers.
30. **Inherit:** have.
33. **stand in number:** be one of the crowd (of girls). **though in reck'ning none:** though none will be worth more than Juliet is.

To SERVANT, *giving him a paper.*

Go, sirrah, trudge about
Through fair Verona; find those persons out   35
Whose names are written there, and to them say
My house and welcome on their pleasure stay.°

Exit with PARIS.

Servant. Find them out whose names are written here?
It is written that the shoemaker should meddle with
his yard and the tailor with his last, the fisher with   40
his pencil and the painter with his nets;° but I
am sent to find those persons whose names are here
writ, and can never find° what names the writing
person hath here writ. I must to the learned. In good
time!°   45

Enter BENVOLIO *and* ROMEO.

Benvolio.
Tut, man, one fire burns out another's burning;
    One pain is less'ned by another's anguish;
Turn giddy, and be holp by backward turning;°
    One desperate grief cures with another's languish.
Take thou some new infection to thy eye,   50
And the rank poison of the old will die.

Romeo.
Your plantain leaf is excellent for that.

Benvolio.
For what, I pray thee?

Romeo.   For your broken° shin.

---

37.   **stay:** wait.
39–41.   **shoemaker . . . nets:** The servant is mixing up several proverbs.
        He's trying to say that people should attend to what they do best.
43.   **find:** know.
44–45.   **In good time!:** Just in time!
48.   **be holp by backward turning:** be helped by turning in the opposite
        direction.
53.   **broken:** damaged.

Benvolio.

Why, Romeo, art thou mad?

Romeo.

Not mad, but bound more than a madman is;   55

Shut up in prison, kept without my food,

Whipped and tormented and—God-den,° good fellow.

Servant. God gi' go-den. I pray, sir, can you read?

Romeo.

Ay, mine own fortune in my misery.

Servant. Perhaps you have learned it without book. But,   60

I pray, can you read anything you see?

Romeo.

Ay, if I know the letters and the language.

Servant. Ye say honestly. Rest you merry.

Romeo. Stay, fellow; I can read.

He reads the letter.

"Signior Martino and his wife and daughters;   65

County Anselm and his beauteous sisters;

The lady widow of Vitruvio;

Signior Placentio and his lovely nieces;

Mercutio and his brother Valentine;

Mine uncle Capulet, his wife and daughters;   70

My fair niece Rosaline; Livia;

Signior Valentio and his cousin Tybalt;

Lucio and the lively Helena."

A fair assembly. Whither should they come?

Servant. Up.   75

Romeo. Whither? To supper?

Servant. To our house.

Romeo. Whose house?

Servant. My master's.

Romeo.

Indeed I should have asked you that before.   80

---

57. **God-den:** good evening.

Servant. Now I'll tell you without asking. My master is
the great rich Capulet; and if you be not of the house
of Montagues, I pray come and crush a cup of wine.
Rest you merry.

Exit.

Benvolio.

At this same ancient° feast of Capulet's   85
Sups the fair Rosaline whom thou so loves;
With all the admirèd beauties of Verona.
Go thither, and with unattainted° eye
Compare her face with some that I shall show,
And I will make thee think thy swan a crow.   90

Romeo.

When the devout religion of mine eye
    Maintains such falsehood, then turn tears to fires;
And these, who, often drowned, could never die,
    Transparent heretics,° be burnt for liars!
One fairer than my love? The all-seeing sun   95
Ne'er saw her match since first the world begun.

Benvolio.

Tut! you saw her fair, none else being by,
Herself poised° with herself in either eye;
But in that crystal scales° let there be weighed
Your lady's love against some other maid   100
That I will show you shining at this feast,
And she shall scant° show well that now seems best.

Romeo.

I'll go along, no such sight to be shown,
But to rejoice in splendor of mine own.

Exeunt.

---

85. **ancient:** old; established by an old custom.
88. **unattainted:** untainted (by prejudice).
94. **Transparent heretics:** His eyes would be easily "seen through"—they
    would betray the truth.
98. **poised:** balanced (for comparison).
99. **crystal scales:** Romeo's eyes.
102. **scant:** hardly.

Scene 3. *A room in Capulet's house.*

Enter Capulet's wife, LADY CAPULET, *and* NURSE.

Lady Capulet.
Nurse, where's my daughter? Call her forth to me.
Nurse.
Now, by my maidenhead at twelve year old,
I bade her come. What,° lamb! What, ladybird!
God forbid, where's this girl? What, Juliet!

Enter JULIET.

Juliet.
How now? Who calls?
Nurse.   Your mother.
Juliet.   Madam, I am here.   5
What is your will?
Lady Capulet.
This is the matter.—Nurse, give leave awhile;
We must talk in secret. Nurse, come back again.
I have rememb'red me; thou's° hear our counsel.
Thou knowest my daughter's of a pretty age.   10
Nurse.
Faith, I can tell her age unto an hour.
Lady Capulet.
She's not fourteen.
Nurse.   I'll lay fourteen of my teeth—
And yet, to my teen° be it spoken, I have but four—
She's not fourteen. How long is it now
To Lammastide?°
Lady Capulet.   A fortnight and odd days.   15
Nurse.
Even or odd, of all days in the year,
Come Lammas Eve at night shall she be fourteen.

I.3.3.   **What:** a call, like "Hey!" or "Where are you?"
   9.   **thou's:** thou shalt.
 13.   **teen:** sorrow.
 15.   **Lammastide:** church feast, on August 1.

Susan and she (God rest all Christian souls!)
Were of an age.° Well, Susan is with God;
She was too good for me. But, as I said,   20
On Lammas Eve at night shall she be fourteen;
That shall she, marry; I remember it well.
'Tis since the earthquake now eleven years;
And she was weaned (I never shall forget it),
Of all the days of the year, upon that day;   25
For I had then laid wormwood to my dug,°
Sitting in the sun under the dovehouse wall.
My lord and you were then at Mantua.
Nay, I do bear a brain. But, as I said,
When it did taste the wormwood on the nipple   30
Of my dug and felt it bitter, pretty fool,
To see it tetchy° and fall out with the dug!
Shake, quoth the dovehouse!° 'Twas no need, I trow,
To bid me trudge.
And since that time it is eleven years,   35
For then she could stand high-lone;° nay, by th'
   rood,°
She could have run and waddled all about;
For even the day before, she broke her brow;
And then my husband (God be with his soul!
'A was a merry man) took up the child.   40
"Yea," quoth he, "dost thou fall upon thy face?
Thou wilt fall backward when thou hast more wit;°
Wilt thou not, Jule?" and, by my holidam,°
The pretty wretch left crying and said, "Ay."

---

19. **Were of an age:** were the same age.
26. **laid wormwood to my dug:** applied a bitter substance (wormwood) to her breast to wean the baby.
32. **tetchy:** angry.
33. **Shake, quoth the dovehouse:** The dovehouse shook (from the earthquake).
36. **high-lone:** unaided. **by th' rood:** by the cross (a mild oath).
42. **wit:** understanding.
43. **by my holidam:** by my holy relic (object associated with a saint).

To see now how a jest shall come about! 45
I warrant, and I should live a thousand years,
I never should forget it. "Wilt thou not, Jule?" quoth
   he,
And, pretty fool, it stinted° and said, "Ay."
Lady Capulet.
Enough of this. I pray thee hold thy peace.
Nurse.
Yes, madam. Yet I cannot choose but laugh 50
To think it should leave crying and say, "Ay."
And yet, I warrant, it had upon its brow
A bump as big as a young cock'rel's stone;
A perilous knock; and it cried bitterly.
"Yea," quoth my husband, "fall'st upon thy face? 55
Thou wilt fall backward when thou comest to age,
Wilt thou not, Jule?" It stinted and said, "Ay."
Juliet.
And stint thou too, I pray thee, nurse, say I.
Nurse.
Peace, I have done. God mark thee to his grace!
Thou wast the prettiest babe that e'er I nursed. 60
And I might live to see thee married once,
I have my wish.
Lady Capulet.
Marry, that "marry" is the very theme
I came to talk of. Tell me, daughter Juliet,
How stands your disposition to be married? 65
Juliet.
It is an honor that I dream not of.
Nurse.
An honor? Were not I thine only nurse,
I would say thou hadst sucked wisdom from thy teat.
Lady Capulet.
Well, think of marriage now. Younger than you,
Here in Verona, ladies of esteem, 70

---

48. stinted: stopped.

Are made already mothers. By my count,
I was your mother much upon these years
That you are now a maid. Thus then in brief:
The valiant Paris seeks you for his love.

Nurse.
A man, young lady! Lady, such a man   75
As all the world.—Why, he's a man of wax.°

Lady Capulet.
Verona's summer hath not such a flower.

Nurse.
Nay, he's a flower, in faith—a very flower.

Lady Capulet.
What say you? Can you love the gentleman?
This night you shall behold him at our feast.   80
Read o'er the volume of young Paris' face,
And find delight writ there with beauty's pen;
Examine every married lineament,°
And see how one another lends content;°
And what obscured in this fair volume lies   85
Find written in the margent of his eyes.
This precious book of love, this unbound lover,
To beautify him only lacks a cover.
The fish lives in the sea, and 'tis much pride
For fair without the fair within to hide.°   90
That book in many's eyes doth share the glory,
That in gold clasps locks in the golden story;
So shall you share all that he doth possess,
By having him, making yourself no less.

Nurse.
No less? Nay, bigger! Women grow by men.   95

---

76. **man of wax:** man like a wax statue, with a perfect figure.
83. **married lineament:** perfectly united part.
84. **how one another lends content:** how one feature makes another look good.
90. **For fair without the fair within to hide:** for those who are handsome outwardly to also be handsome inwardly.

Lady Capulet.
Speak briefly, can you like of Paris' love?
Juliet.
I'll look to like, if looking liking move;
But no more deep will I endart mine eye
Than your consent gives strength to make it fly.

Enter SERVINGMAN.

Servingman. Madam, the guests are come, supper   100
served up, you called, my young lady asked for, the
nurse cursed in the pantry, and everything in ex-
tremity. I must hence to wait. I beseech you follow
straight.

Exit.

Lady Capulet.
We follow thee. Juliet, the county stays.°   105
Nurse.
Go, girl, seek happy nights to happy days.

Exeunt.

Scene 4. *A street.*

Enter ROMEO, MERCUTIO, BENVOLIO, *with five or six other*
MASKERS; TORCHBEARERS.

Romeo.
What, shall this speech be spoke for our excuse?°
Or shall we on without apology?

---

105. **the county stays:** the count waits.
I.4.1. **shall this speech be spoke for our excuse?:** shall we introduce
ourselves with the usual speeches? (Uninvited maskers were usually
announced by a messenger.)

Benvolio.
> The date is out of such prolixity.°
> We'll have no Cupid hoodwinked° with a scarf,
> Bearing a Tartar's painted bow of lath,   5
> Scaring the ladies like a crowkeeper;°
> Nor no without-book prologue,° faintly spoke
> After the prompter, for our entrance;
> But, let them measure° us by what they will,
> We'll measure them a measure° and be gone.   10

Romeo.
> Give me a torch. I am not for this ambling.
> Being but heavy, I will bear the light.

Mercutio.
> Nay, gentle Romeo, we must have you dance.

Romeo.
> Not I, believe me. You have dancing shoes
> With nimble soles; I have a soul of lead   15
> So stakes me to the ground I cannot move.

Mercutio.
> You are a lover. Borrow Cupid's wings
> And soar with them above a common bound.

Romeo.
> I am too sore enpiercèd with his shaft
> To soar with his light feathers; and so bound   20
> I cannot bound a pitch° above dull woe.
> Under love's heavy burden do I sink.

Mercutio.
> And, to sink in it, should you burden love—
> Too great oppression for a tender thing.

---

3. **The date is out of such prolixity:** Such long-winded speeches are out of fashion now.
4. **hoodwinked:** blindfolded.
6. **crowkeeper:** scarecrow.
7. **without-book prologue:** speech delivered from memory.
9. **measure:** examine.
10. **measure them a measure:** dance one dance.
21. **bound a pitch:** leap as high as a falcon.

Romeo.

Is love a tender thing? It is too rough,   25
Too rude, too boist'rous, and it pricks like thorn.

Mercutio.

If love be rough with you, be rough with love;
Prick love for pricking, and you beat love down.
Give me a case to put my visage in.
A visor° for a visor! What care I   30
What curious eye doth quote deformities?°
Here are the beetle brows shall blush° for me.

Benvolio.

Come, knock and enter; and no sooner in
But every man betake him to his legs.°

Romeo.

A torch for me! Let wantons light of heart   35
Tickle the senseless rushes° with their heels;
For I am proverbed with a grandsire phrase,°
I'll be a candleholder and look on;
The game was ne'er so fair, and I am done.°

Mercutio.

Tut! Dun's the mouse, the constable's own word!   40
If thou art Dun,° we'll draw thee from the mire
Of this sir-reverence love,° wherein thou stickest
Upon to the ears. Come, we burn daylight, ho!

---

30. **visor:** mask.
31. **quote deformities:** see imperfections (in the way he looks).
32. **Here are the beetle brows shall blush:** The mask's heavy eyebrows will blush for him.
34. **betake him to his legs:** begin to dance.
36. **rushes:** The dance floor is covered with rushes.
37. **grandsire phrase:** old man's saying.
39. **The game ... I am done:** The game (dancing) was never very good, and I'm exhausted.
41. **Dun:** pun on Romeo's "done"; Dun was the common name used for a horse in an old game called "Dun is in the mire."
42. **sir-reverence love:** "Save your reverence" is an apologetic expression. Mercutio means "We'll save you from—pardon me for saying so—love."

Romeo.
    Nay, that's not so.
Mercutio.   I mean, sir, in delay
    We waste our lights° in vain, like lights by day.   45
    Take our good meaning, for our judgment sits
    Five times in that° ere once in our five wits.
Romeo.
    And we mean well in going to this masque,
    But 'tis no wit° to go.
Mercutio.   Why, may one ask?
Romeo.
    I dreamt a dream tonight.
Mercutio.   And so did I.   50
Romeo.
    Well, what was yours?
Mercutio.   That dreamers often lie.
Romeo.
    In bed asleep, while they do dream things true.
Mercutio.
    O, then I see Queen Mab hath been with you.
    She is the fairies' midwife, and she comes
    In shape no bigger than an agate stone   55
    On the forefinger of an alderman,
    Drawn with a team of little atomies°
    Over men's noses as they lie asleep;
    Her wagon spokes made of long spinners'° legs,
    The cover, of the wings of grasshoppers;   60
    Her traces,° of the smallest spider web;
    Her collars, of the moonshine's wat'ry beams;
    Her whip, of cricket's bone; the lash, of film;°
    Her wagoner, a small gray-coated gnat,

---

45. **lights:** torches.
47. **in that:** in our good meaning.
49. **no wit:** not a good idea.
57. **atomies:** tiny creatures.
59. **spinners':** spiders'.
61. **traces:** reins and harnesses for a wagon.
63. **film:** filament, or thread.

Not half so big as a round little worm   65
Pricked from the lazy finger of a maid;°
Her chariot is an empty hazelnut,
Made by the joiner squirrel or old grub,
Time out o' mind the fairies' coachmakers.
And in this state she gallops night by night   70
Through lovers' brains, and then they dream of love;
On courtiers' knees, that dream on curtsies straight;
O'er lawyers' fingers, who straight dream on fees;
O'er ladies' lips, who straight on kisses dream,
Which oft the angry Mab with blisters plagues,   75
Because their breaths with sweetmeats tainted are.
Sometime she gallops o'er a courtier's nose,
And then dreams he of smelling out a suit;°
And sometime comes she with a tithe pig's° tail
Tickling a parson's nose as 'a lies asleep,   80
Then dreams he of another benefice.°
Sometime she driveth o'er a soldier's neck,
And then dreams he of cutting foreign throats,
Of breaches, ambuscadoes, Spanish blades,
Of healths° five fathom deep; and then anon   85
Drums in his ear, at which he starts and wakes,
And being thus frighted, swears a prayer or two
And sleeps again. This is that very Mab
That plaits the manes of horses in the night
And bakes the elflocks° in foul sluttish hairs,   90
Which once untangled much misfortune bodes.
This is the hag,° when maids lie on their backs,
That presses them and learns them first to bear,

---

66. **lazy finger of a maid:** Lazy maids were said to have worms growing in their fingers.
78. **suit:** person who might want to buy his influence at court.
79. **tithe pig's:** A tithe is a tenth of one's income given to the church. Farmers often gave the parson one pig as a tithe.
81. **benefice:** church office that enabled a minister to make a living.
85. **healths:** toasts to his health.
90. **elflocks:** locks of hair that were tangled by mischievous elves.
92. **hag:** nightmare. Nightmares were thought to be spirits who molested women at night.

Making them women of good carriage.°
This is she——

Romeo.   Peace, peace, Mercutio, peace!   95
Thou talk'st of nothing.

Mercutio.   True, I talk of dreams;
Which are the children of an idle brain,
Begot of nothing but vain fantasy;
Which is as thin of substance as the air,
And more inconstant than the wind, who woos   100
Even now the frozen bosom of the North
And, being angered, puffs away from thence,
Turning his side to the dewdropping South.

Benvolio.
This wind you talk of blows us from ourselves.
Supper is done, and we shall come too late.   105

Romeo.
I fear, too early; for my mind misgives
Some consequence yet hanging in the stars
Shall bitterly begin his fearful date
With this night's revels and expire the term
Of a despisèd life, closed in my breast,   110
By some vile forfeit of untimely death.
But he that hath the steerage of my course
Direct my sail! On, lusty gentlemen!

Benvolio. Strike, drum.

They march about the stage, and retire to one side.

Scene 5. *A hall in Capulet's house.*

SERVINGMEN *come forth with napkins.*

First Servingman. Where's Potpan, that he helps not
to take away? He shift a trencher!° He scrape a
trencher!

---

94. **women of good carriage:** women who can bear children well.
I.5.2. **trencher:** wooden platter.

Second Servingman. When good manners shall lie all
in one or two men's hands, and they unwashed too,   5
'tis a foul thing.
First Servingman. Away with the join-stools,° remove
the court cupboard, look to the plate. Good thou,
save me a piece of marchpane,° and as thou loves
me, let the porter let in Susan Grindstone and Nell,   10
Anthony, and Potpan!
Second Servingman. Ay, boy, ready.
First Servingman. You are looked for and called for,
asked for and sought for, in the great chamber.
Third Servingman. We cannot be here and there too.   15
Cheerly, boys! Be brisk awhile, and the longer liver
take all.

Exeunt.

Enter CAPULET, LADY CAPULET, JULIET, TYBALT, NURSE, *and all
the* GUESTS *and* GENTLEWOMEN, *meeting the maskers.*

Capulet.
Welcome, gentlemen! Ladies that have their toes
Unplagued with corns will walk a bout° with you.
Ah, my mistresses, which of you all   20
Will now deny to dance? She that makes dainty,°
She I'll swear hath corns. Am I come near ye now?
Welcome, gentlemen! I have seen the day
That I have worn a visor and could tell
A whispering tale in a fair lady's ear,   25
Such as would please. 'Tis gone, 'tis gone, 'tis gone.
You are welcome, gentlemen! Come, musicians, play.

Music plays, and they dance.

A hall,° a hall! Give room! And foot it, girls.
More light, you knaves, and turn the tables up,

---

7. **join-stools:** wooden stools made by a carpenter (a joiner).
9. **marchpane:** marzipan.
19. **bout:** dance.
21. **makes dainty:** pretends to be shy.
28. **A hall:** clear the hall (for dancing).

And quench the fire; the room is grown too hot.   30
Ah, sirrah, this unlooked-for sport° comes well.
Nay, sit; nay, sit, good cousin Capulet;
For you and I are past our dancing days.
How long is't now since last yourself and I
Were in a mask?
Second Capulet.   By'r Lady, thirty years.   35
Capulet.
   What, man? 'Tis not so much, 'tis not so much;
   'Tis since the nuptial of Lucentio,
   Come Pentecost as quickly as it will,
   Some five-and-twenty years, and then we masked.
Second Capulet.
   'Tis more, 'tis more. His son is elder, sir;   40
   His son is thirty.
Capulet.   Will you tell me that?
   His son was but a ward° two years ago.
Romeo [*to a* SERVINGMAN].
   What lady's that which doth enrich the hand
   Of yonder knight?
Servingman. I know not, sir.   45
Romeo.
   O, she doth teach the torches to burn bright!
   It seems she hangs upon the cheek of night
   As a rich jewel in an Ethiop's ear—
   Beauty too rich for use, for earth too dear!
   So shows a snowy dove trooping with crows   50
   As yonder lady o'er her fellows shows.
   The measure° done, I'll watch her place of stand
   And, touching hers, make blessèd my rude° hand.
   Did my heart love till now? Forswear it, sight!
   For I ne'er saw true beauty till this night.   55

---

31. **unlooked-for sport:** He hadn't expected to find some of the dancers
    masked.
42. **ward:** minor.
52. **measure:** dance.
53. **rude:** rough or simple.

Tybalt.
    This, by his voice, should be a Montague.
    Fetch me my rapier, boy. What! Dares the slave
    Come hither, covered with an antic face,°
    To fleer° and scorn at our solemnity?
    Now, by the stock and honor of my kin,   60
    To strike him dead I hold it not a sin.
Capulet.
    Why, how now, kinsman? Wherefore storm you so?
Tybalt.
    Uncle, this is a Montague, our foe,
    A villain, that is hither come in spite
    To scorn at our solemnity this night.   65
Capulet.
    Young Romeo is it?
Tybalt.   'Tis he, that villain Romeo.
Capulet.
    Content thee, gentle coz, let him alone.
    'A bears him like a portly° gentleman,
    And, to say truth, Verona brags of him
    To be a virtuous and well-governed youth.   70
    I would not for the wealth of all this town
    Here in my house do him disparagement.
    Therefore be patient; take no note of him.
    It is my will, the which if thou respect,
    Show a fair presence and put off these frowns,   75
    An ill-beseeming semblance for a feast.
Tybalt.
    It fits when such a villain is a guest.
    I'll not endure him.
Capulet.   He shall be endured.
    What, goodman boy!° I say he shall. Go to!°

---

58. antic face: grotesque mask.
59. fleer: sneer.
68. portly: well-behaved.
79. goodman boy: a scornful phrase. *Goodman* is below the rank of
gentleman; *boy* is insulting. **Go to!:** similar to "Go on!" or "Cut it out!"

Am I the master here, or you? Go to!   80
You'll not endure him, God shall mend my soul!
You'll make a mutiny among my guests!
You will set cock-a-hoop.° You'll be the man!
Tybalt.
Why, uncle, 'tis a shame.
Capulet.   Go to, go to!
You are a saucy boy. Is't so, indeed?   85
This trick may chance to scathe° you. I know what.
You must contrary me! Marry, 'tis time —
Well said, my hearts!—You are a princox°—go!
Be quiet, or—More light, more light!—For shame!
I'll make you quiet. What!—Cheerly, my hearts!   90
Tybalt.
Patience perforce° with willful choler meeting
Makes my flesh tremble in their different greeting.
I will withdraw; but this intrusion shall,
Now seeming sweet, convert to bitt'rest gall.

                                                Exit.

Romeo.
If I profane with my unworthiest hand   95
   This holy shrine, the gentle sin is this:°
My lips, two blushing pilgrims, ready stand
   To smooth that rough touch with a tender kiss.
Juliet.
Good pilgrim, you do wrong your hand too much,
   Which mannerly devotion shows in this;   100
For saints have hands that pilgrims' hands do touch,
   And palm to palm is holy palmers'° kiss.

---

83. **set cock-a-hoop:** start trouble.
86. **scathe:** injure.
88. **princox:** conceited boy.
91. **Patience perforce:** enforced patience.
96. **the gentle sin is this:** this is the sin of a gentleman.
102. **palmers':** pilgrims going to a holy place. They often carried palm
      leaves to show they had been to the Holy Land.

Romeo.
Have not saints lips, and holy palmers too?
Juliet.
Ay, pilgrim, lips that they must use in prayer.
Romeo.
O, then, dear saint, let lips do what hands do!   105
They pray; grant thou, lest faith turn to despair.
Juliet.
Saints do not move,° though grant for prayers' sake.
Romeo.
Then move not while my prayer's effect I take.
Thus from my lips, by thine my sin is purged.

Kisses her.

Juliet.
Then have my lips the sin that they have took.   110
Romeo.
Sin from my lips? O trespass sweetly urged!
Give me my sin again. [*Kisses her.*]
Juliet.   You kiss by th' book.°
Nurse.
Madam, your mother craves a word with you.
Romeo.
What is her mother?
Nurse.   Marry, bachelor,
Her mother is the lady of the house,   115
And a good lady, and a wise and virtuous.
I nursed her daughter that you talked withal.°
I tell you, he that can lay hold of her
Shall have the chinks.°
Romeo.   Is she a Capulet?
O dear account! My life is my foe's debt.°   120

---

107. **do not move:** do not make the first move.
112. **You kiss by th' book:** You take me literally (to get more kisses).
117. **withal:** with.
119. **chinks:** money.
120. **is my foe's debt:** belongs to my enemy.

Benvolio.

Away, be gone; the sport is at the best.

Romeo.

Ay, so I fear; the more is my unrest.

Capulet.

Nay, gentlemen, prepare not to be gone;
We have a trifling foolish banquet towards.°
Is it e'en so? Why then, I thank you all.   125
I thank you, honest gentlemen. Good night.
More torches here! Come on then; let's to bed.
Ah, sirrah, by my fay,° it waxes late;
I'll to my rest.

Exeunt all but JULIET *and* NURSE.

Juliet.

Come hither, nurse. What is yond gentleman?   130

Nurse.

The son and heir of old Tiberio.

Juliet.

What's he that now is going out of door?

Nurse.

Marry, that, I think, be young Petruchio.

Juliet.

What's he that follows there, that would not dance?

Nurse. I know not.   135

Juliet.

Go ask his name.—If he be marrièd,
My grave is like to be my wedding bed.

Nurse.

His name is Romeo, and a Montague,
The only son of your great enemy.

---

124. **towards:** coming up.
128. **fay:** faith.

Juliet.
>My only love, sprung from my only hate!   140
>Too early seen unknown, and known too late!
>Prodigious° birth of love it is to me
>That I must love a loathèd enemy.

Nurse.
>What's this? What's this?

Juliet.   A rhyme I learnt even now
>Of one I danced withal.

One calls within, "Juliet."

Nurse.   Anon, anon!°   145
>Come, let's away; the strangers all are gone.

>>>>>>>>*Exeunt.*

---

142. **Prodigious:** huge and monstrous.
145. **anon:** now.

Act II

Enter CHORUS.

Chorus.
Now old desire doth in his deathbed lie,
  And young affection gapes to be his heir;
That fair° for which love groaned for and would die,
  With tender Juliet matched, is now not fair.
Now Romeo is beloved and loves again,   5
  Alike° bewitchèd by the charm of looks;
But to his foe supposed he must complain,°
  And she steal love's sweet bait from fearful hooks.
Being held a foe, he may not have access
  To breathe such vows as lovers use to swear,°   10
And she as much in love, her means much less
  To meet her new belovèd anywhere;
But passion lends them power, time means, to meet,
Temp'ring extremities° with extreme sweet.° [*Exit.*]

Scene 1. *Near Capulet's orchard.*

Enter ROMEO *alone.*

Romeo.
Can I go forward when my heart is here?
Turn back, dull earth, and find thy center° out.

Chor. 3.   That fair: Rosaline.
  6.   Alike: both (both Romeo and Juliet).
  7.   complain: ask Juliet's father, his foe, for her hand in marriage.
10.   use to swear: are used to promising.
14.   extremities: difficulties. **extreme sweet:** very sweet delights.
II.1.2.   center: Juliet. The "dull earth" is Romeo, and Juliet is his soul.

Enter BENVOLIO *with* MERCUTIO. ROMEO *retires.*

Benvolio.
    Romeo! My cousin Romeo! Romeo!
Mercutio.   He is wise
    And, on my life, hath stol'n him home to bed.
Benvolio.
    He ran this way and leapt this orchard wall.   5
    Call, good Mercutio.
Mercutio.   Nay, I'll conjure too.
    Romeo! Humors! Madman! Passion! Lover!
    Appear thou in the likeness of a sigh;
    Speak but one rhyme, and I am satisfied!
    Cry but "Ay me!" pronounce but "love" and "dove";   10
    Speak to my gossip° Venus one fair word,
    One nickname for her purblind° son and heir,
    Young Abraham Cupid,° he that shot so true
    When King Cophetua loved the beggar maid!°
    He heareth not, he stirreth not, he moveth not;   15
    The ape is dead,° and I must conjure him.
    I conjure thee by Rosaline's bright eyes,
    By her high forehead and her scarlet lip,
    By her fine foot, straight leg, and quivering thigh,
    And the demesnes° that there adjacent lie,   20
    That in thy likeness thou appear to us!
Benvolio.
    And if he hear thee, thou wilt anger him.
Mercutio.
    This cannot anger him. 'Twould anger him
    To raise a spirit in his mistress' circle°

---

11. **gossip:** good friend. Venus is the goddess of love.
12. **purblind:** blind.
13. **Young Abraham Cupid:** To Mercutio, Romeo seems the very figure of love—old like Abraham in the Bible and young like Cupid.
14. **When . . . maid:** from a popular ballad.
16. **The ape is dead:** Romeo is playing dead.
20. **demesnes:** regions.
24. **circle:** magical place.

Of some strange nature, letting it there stand   25
Till she had laid it and conjured it down.
That were some spite;° my invocation
Is fair and honest: in his mistress' name,
I conjure only but to raise up him.
Benvolio.
Come, he hath hid himself among these trees   30
To be consorted° with the humorous° night.
Blind is his love and best befits the dark.
Mercutio.
If love be blind, love cannot hit the mark.
And wish his mistress were that kind of fruit
As maids call medlars when they laugh alone.   35
O, Romeo, that she were, O that she were
An open et cetera, thou a pop'rin pear!
Romeo, good night. I'll to my truckle bed;
This field bed is too cold for me to sleep.
Come, shall we go?
Benvolio.   Go then, for 'tis in vain   40
To seek him here that means not to be found.

Exit with others.

Scene 2. *Capulet's orchard.*

Romeo [*coming forward*].
⤆ He jests at scars that never felt a wound.

Enter JULIET *at a window.*

But soft! What light through yonder window breaks?
It is the East, and Juliet is the sun!

---

27. **spite:** cause to be angry.
31. **consorted:** familiar. **humorous:** damp.

Arise, fair sun, and kill the envious moon,
Who is already sick and pale with grief 5
That thou her maid° art far more fair than she.
Be not her maid, since she is envious.
Her vestal livery° is but sick and green,°
And none but fools do wear it. Cast it off.
It is my lady! O, it is my love! 10
O, that she knew she were!
She speaks, yet she says nothing. What of that?
Her eye discourses;° I will answer it.
I am too bold; 'tis not to me she speaks.
Two of the fairest stars in all the heaven, 15
Having some business, do entreat her eyes
To twinkle in their spheres till they return.
What if her eyes were there, they in her head?
The brightness of her cheek would shame those stars
As daylight doth a lamp; her eyes in heaven 20
Would through the airy region stream so bright
That birds would sing and think it were not night.
See how she leans her cheek upon her hand!
O, that I were a glove upon that hand,
That I might touch that cheek!
Juliet.   Ay me!
Romeo.   She speaks. 25
O, speak again, bright angel, for thou art
As glorious to this night, being o'er my head,
As is a wingèd messenger of heaven
Unto the white-upturnèd wond'ring eyes
Of mortals that fall back to gaze on him 30
When he bestrides the lazy puffing clouds
And sails upon the bosom of the air.

II.2.6. **thou her maid:** Juliet, whom Romeo sees as the servant of the virgin
goddess of the moon, Diana.
 8. **vestal livery:** maidenly clothing. **sick and green:** Unmarried girls
supposedly had "greensickness," or anemia.
13. **discourses:** speaks.

Juliet.

    O Romeo, Romeo! Wherefore art thou Romeo?°
    Deny thy father and refuse thy name;
    Or, if thou wilt not, be but sworn my love,   35
    And I'll no longer be a Capulet.

Romeo [*aside*].

    Shall I hear more, or shall I speak at this?

Juliet.

    'Tis but thy name that is my enemy.
    Thou art thyself, though not° a Montague.
    What's Montague? It is nor hand, nor foot,   40
    Nor arm, nor face. O, be some other name
    Belonging to a man.
    What's in a name? That which we call a rose
    By any other word would smell as sweet.
    So Romeo would, were he not Romeo called,   45
    Retain that dear perfection which he owes°
    Without that title. Romeo, doff thy name;
    And for thy name, which is no part of thee,
    Take all myself.

Romeo.   I take thee at thy word.

    Call me but love, and I'll be new baptized;   50
    Henceforth I never will be Romeo.

Juliet.

    What man art thou, that, thus bescreened in night,
    So stumblest on my counsel?°

Romeo.   By a name

    I know not how to tell thee who I am.
    My name, dear saint, is hateful to myself   55
    Because it is an enemy to thee.
    Had I it written, I would tear the word.

---

33. In other words, "Why is your name Romeo?" (It is the name of her enemy.)
39. **though not:** even if you were not.
46. **owes:** owns.
53. **counsel:** private thoughts.

Juliet.
My ears have yet not drunk a hundred words
Of thy tongue's uttering, yet I know the sound.
Art thou not Romeo, and a Montague?   60
Romeo.
Neither, fair maid, if either thee dislike.
Juliet.
How camest thou hither, tell me, and wherefore?
The orchard walls are high and hard to climb,
And the place death, considering who thou art,
If any of my kinsmen find thee here.   65
Romeo.
With love's light wings did I o'erperch° these walls;
For stony limits cannot hold love out,
And what love can do, that dares love attempt.
Therefore thy kinsmen are no stop to me.
Juliet.
If they do see thee, they will murder thee.   70
Romeo.
Alack, there lies more peril in thine eye
Than twenty of their swords! Look thou but sweet,
And I am proof° against their enmity.
Juliet.
I would not for the world they saw thee here.
Romeo.
I have night's cloak to hide me from their eyes;   75
And but° thou love me, let them find me here.
My life were better ended by their hate
Than death proroguèd,° wanting of thy love.
Juliet.
By whose direction found'st thou out this place?

---

66. **o'erperch:** climb over.
73. **proof:** armored.
76. **but:** if only.
78. **proroguèd:** postponed.

Romeo.

By Love, that first did prompt me to inquire.　　　　80
He lent me counsel, and I lent him eyes.
I am no pilot; yet, wert thou as far
As that vast shore washed with the farthest sea,
I should adventure for such merchandise.

Juliet.

Thou knowest the mask of night is on my face;　　　85
Else would a maiden blush bepaint my cheek
For that which thou hast heard me speak tonight.
Fain would I dwell on form—fain, fain deny
What I have spoke; but farewell compliment.°
Dost thou love me? I know thou wilt say "Ay";　　90
And I will take thy word. Yet, if thou swear'st,
Thou mayst prove false. At lovers' perjuries,
They say Jove laughs. O gentle Romeo,
If thou dost love, pronounce it faithfully.
Or if thou think'st I am too quickly won,　　　　95
I'll frown and be perverse and say thee nay,
So thou wilt woo; but else, not for the world.
In truth, fair Montague, I am too fond,°
And therefore thou mayst think my havior° light;
But trust me, gentleman, I'll prove more true　　100
Than those that have more cunning to be strange.°
I should have been more strange, I must confess,
But that thou overheard'st, ere I was ware,
My truelove passion. Therefore pardon me,
And not impute this yielding to light love,　　　105
Which the dark night hath so discoverèd.°

Romeo.

Lady, by yonder blessèd moon I vow,
That tips with silver all these fruit-tree tops——

---

89. **compliment:** good manners.
98. **fond:** foolishly affectionate.
99. **havior:** behavior.
101. **strange:** cold, distant.
106. **discoverèd:** revealed.

Juliet.

O, swear not by the moon, the inconstant moon,
That monthly changes in her circle orb,   110
Lest that thy love prove likewise variable.

Romeo.

What shall I swear by?

Juliet.   Do not swear at all;
Or if thou wilt, swear by thy gracious self,
Which is the god of my idolatry,
And I'll believe thee.

Romeo.   If my heart's dear love——   115

Juliet.

Well, do not swear. Although I joy in thee,
I have no joy of this contract tonight.
It is too rash, too unadvised, too sudden;
Too like the lightning, which doth cease to be
Ere one can say it lightens. Sweet, good night!   120
This bud of love, by summer's ripening breath,
May prove a beauteous flower when next we meet.
Good night, good night! As sweet repose and rest
Come to thy heart as that within my breast!

Romeo.

O, wilt thou leave me so unsatisfied?   125

Juliet.

What satisfaction canst thou have tonight?

Romeo.

The exchange of thy love's faithful vow for mine.

Juliet.

I gave thee mine before thou didst request it;
And yet I would it were to give again.

Romeo.

Wouldst thou withdraw it? For what purpose, love?   130

Juliet.

But to be frank° and give it thee again.
And yet I wish but for the thing I have.

---

131. **frank:** open and true.

My bounty° is as boundless as the sea,
My love as deep; the more I give to thee,
The more I have, for both are infinite.   135
I hear some noise within. Dear love, adieu!

NURSE *calls within.*

Anon, good nurse! Sweet Montague, be true.
Stay but a little, I will come again.   [*Exit.*]
Romeo.
O blessèd, blessèd night! I am afeard,
Being in night, all this is but a dream,   140
Too flattering-sweet to be substantial.

Enter JULIET *again.*

Juliet.
Three words, dear Romeo, and good night indeed.
If that thy bent° of love be honorable,
Thy purpose marriage, send me word tomorrow,
By one that I'll procure to come to thee,   145
Where and what time thou wilt perform the rite;
And all my fortunes at thy foot I'll lay
And follow thee my lord throughout the world.
Nurse [*within*]. Madam!
Juliet.
I come anon.—But if thou meanest not well,   150
I do beseech thee——
Nurse [*within*]. Madam!
Juliet.   By and by I come.—
To cease thy strife° and leave me to my grief.
Tomorrow will I send.
Romeo.   So thrive my soul——
Juliet.
A thousand times good night!   [*Exit.*]   155

---

133. **bounty:** generosity.
143. **bent:** intention.
153. **strife:** efforts to win her.

Romeo.

A thousand times the worse, to want thy light!
Love goes toward love as schoolboys from their books;
But love from love, toward school with heavy looks.

Enter JULIET *again.*

Juliet.

Hist! Romeo, hist! O for a falc'ner's voice
To lure this tassel gentle° back again!   160
Bondage is hoarse° and may not speak aloud,
Else would I tear the cave where Echo° lies
And make her airy tongue more hoarse than mine
With repetition of "My Romeo!"

Romeo.

It is my soul that calls upon my name.   165
How silver-sweet sound lovers' tongues by night,
Like softest music to attending ears!

Juliet.

Romeo!

Romeo.

    My sweet?

Juliet.   What o'clock tomorrow
Shall I send to thee?

Romeo.   By the hour of nine.

Juliet.

I will not fail. 'Tis twenty years till then.   170
I have forgot why I did call thee back.

Romeo.

Let me stand here till thou remember it.

Juliet.

I shall forget, to have thee still stand there,
Rememb'ring how I love thy company.

---

160. **tassel gentle:** male falcon.
161. **Bondage is hoarse:** Juliet is in "bondage" to her parents and must whisper.
162. **Echo:** mythical girl who could only repeat others' final words.

Romeo.
    And I'll still stay, to have thee still forget,   175
    Forgetting any other home but this.
Juliet.
    'Tis almost morning. I would have thee gone—
    And yet no farther than a wanton's° bird,
    That lets it hop a little from his hand,
    Like a poor prisoner in his twisted gyves,°   180
    And with a silken thread plucks it back again,
    So loving-jealous of his liberty.
Romeo.
    I would I were thy bird.
Juliet.   Sweet, so would I.
    Yet I should kill thee with much cherishing.
    Good night, good night! Parting is such sweet sorrow   185
    That I shall say good night till it be morrow.   [*Exit.*]
Romeo.
    Sleep dwell upon thine eyes, peace in thy breast!
    Would I were sleep and peace, so sweet to rest!
    Hence will I to my ghostly friar's° close cell,
    His help to crave and my dear hap° to tell.   [*Exit.*]   190

Scene 3. *Friar Laurence's cell.*

Enter FRIAR LAURENCE *alone, with a basket.*

Friar.
    The gray-eyed morn smiles on the frowning night,
    Check'ring the eastern clouds with streaks of light;
    And fleckèd darkness like a drunkard reels
    From forth day's path and Titan's burning wheels.°

---

178. **wanton's:** careless child's.
180. **gyves:** chains, like the threads that hold the bird captive.
189. **ghostly friar's:** spiritual advisor's.
190. **hap:** luck.
II.3.4. **Titan's burning wheels:** wheels of the sun god's chariot.

Now, ere the sun advance his burning eye   5
The day to cheer and night's dank dew to dry,
I must upfill this osier cage° of ours
With baleful° weeds and precious-juicèd flowers.
The earth that's Nature's mother is her tomb.
What is her burying grave, that is her womb;   10
And from her womb children of divers kind
We sucking on her natural bosom find,
Many for many virtues excellent,
None but for some, and yet all different.
O, mickle° is the powerful grace that lies   15
In plants, herbs, stones, and their true qualities;
For naught so vile that on the earth doth live
But to the earth some special good doth give;
Nor aught so good but, strained° from that fair use,
Revolts from true birth,° stumbling on abuse.   20
Virtue itself turns vice, being misapplied,
And vice sometime by action dignified.

Enter ROMEO.

Within the infant rind° of this weak flower
Poison hath residence and medicine° power;
For this, being smelt, with that part cheers each part;°   25
Being tasted, stays all senses with the heart.
Two such opposèd kings encamp them still°
In man as well as herbs—grace and rude will;
And where the worser is predominant,
Full soon the canker° death eats up that plant.   30

---

  7. **osier cage:** cage woven of willow branches.
  8. **baleful:** poisonous.
 15. **mickle:** great.
 19. **strained:** turned aside.
 20. **true birth:** true purpose.
 23. **rind:** outer covering.
 24. **medicine:** medicinal.
 25. **For . . . part:** When the flower is smelled, each part of the body is
     stimulated.
 27. **still:** always.
 30. **canker:** cankerworm, which feeds on leaves.

Romeo.
Good morrow, father.
Friar.   Benedicite!°
What early tongue so sweet saluteth me?
Young son, it argues a distemperèd head°
So soon to bid good morrow to thy bed.
Care keeps his watch in every old man's eye,   35
And where care lodges, sleep will never lie;
But where unbruisèd° youth with unstuffed° brain
Doth couch his limbs, there golden sleep doth reign.
Therefore thy earliness doth me assure
Thou art uproused with some distemp'rature;   40
Or if not so, then here I hit it right—
Our Romeo hath not been in bed tonight.
Romeo.
That last is true. The sweeter rest was mine.
Friar.
God pardon sin! Wast thou with Rosaline?
Romeo.
With Rosaline, my ghostly father? No.   45
I have forgot that name and that name's woe.
Friar.
That's my good son! But where hast thou been then?
Romeo.
I'll tell thee ere thou ask it me again.
I have been feasting with mine enemy,
Where on a sudden one hath wounded me   50
That's by me wounded. Both our remedies
Within thy help and holy physic° lies.
I bear no hatred, blessèd man, for, lo,
My intercession° likewise steads° my foe.

---

31. **Benedicite!:** Latin for "Bless you!"
33. **distemperèd head:** disturbed mind.
37. **unbruisèd:** innocent. **unstuffed:** calm.
52. **holy physic:** the friar's healing power ("physic") to make Romeo and Juliet husband and wife.
54. **intercession:** request. **steads:** benefits.

Friar.
Be plain, good son, and homely° in thy drift.   55
Riddling confession finds but riddling shrift.°
Romeo.
Then plainly know my heart's dear love is set
On the fair daughter of rich Capulet;
As mine on hers, so hers is set on mine,
And all combined,° save what thou must combine   60
By holy marriage. When and where and how
We met, we wooed, and made exchange of vow,
I'll tell thee as we pass; but this I pray,
That thou consent to marry us today.
Friar.
Holy Saint Francis! What a change is here!   65
Is Rosaline, that thou didst love so dear,
So soon forsaken? Young men's love then lies
Not truly in their hearts, but in their eyes.
Jesu Maria! What a deal of brine
Hath washed thy sallow cheeks for Rosaline!   70
How much salt water thrown away in waste
To season° love, that of it doth not taste!
The sun not yet thy sighs from heaven clears,
Thy old groans ring yet in mine ancient ears.
Lo, here upon thy cheek the stain doth sit   75
Of an old tear that is not washed off yet.
If e'er thou wast thyself, and these woes thine,
Thou and these woes were all for Rosaline.
And art thou changed? Pronounce this sentence then:
Women may fall when there's no strength in men.   80
Romeo.
Thou chid'st me oft for loving Rosaline.

---

55. **homely:** simple and straightforward.
56. **shrift:** forgiveness (in the religious rite of confession).
60. **combined:** agreed.
72. **season:** preserve; keep fresh (food was seasoned with salt to keep it from spoiling).

Friar.
For doting, not for loving, pupil mine.
Romeo.
And bad'st me bury love.
Friar.   Not in a grave
To lay one in, another out to have.
Romeo.
I pray thee chide me not. Her I love now   85
Doth grace° for grace and love for love allow.
The other did not so.
Friar.   O she knew well
Thy love did read by rote, that could not spell.°
But come, young waverer, come go with me.
In one respect I'll thy assistant be;   90
For this alliance may so happy prove
To turn your households' rancor to pure love.
Romeo.
O, let us hence! I stand on° sudden haste.
Friar.
Wisely and slow. They stumble that run fast. [*Exeunt.*]

Scene 4. *A street.*

Enter BENVOLIO *and* MERCUTIO.

Mercutio.
Where the devil should this Romeo be?
Came he not home tonight?
Benvolio.
Not to his father's. I spoke with his man.

---

86. **grace:** favor.
88. Romeo recited words of love without understanding them.
93. **I stand on:** I am firm about.

Mercutio.
Why, that same pale hardhearted wench, that
    Rosaline,
Torments him so that he will sure run mad.   5
Benvolio.
Tybalt, the kinsman to old Capulet,
Hath sent a letter to his father's house.
Mercutio. A challenge, on my life.
Benvolio. Romeo will answer it.
Mercutio. Any man that can write may answer a letter.   10
Benvolio. Nay, he will answer the letter's master, how
he dares, being dared.
Mercutio. Alas, poor Romeo, he is already dead: stabbed
with a white wench's black eye; run through the ear
with a love song; the very pin° of his heart cleft with   15
the blind bow-boy's butt-shaft; and is he a man to
encounter Tybalt?
Benvolio. Why, what is Tybalt?
Mercutio. More than Prince of Cats.° O, he's the coura-
geous captain of compliments. He fights as you sing   20
pricksong°—keeps time, distance, and proportion; he
rests his minim rests,° one, two and the third in
your bosom! The very butcher of a silk button, a
duelist, a duelist! A gentleman of the very first
house,° of the first and second cause.° Ah, the immor-   25
tal passado!° The punto reverso!° The hay!°
Benvolio. The what?

II.4.15.   **pin:** center (of a target).
19.   **Prince of Cats:** Tybalt is the name of a cat in a fable who is known for
his slyness.
20–21.   **sing pricksong:** sing with attention to every note on a printed
sheet of music.
22.   **minim rests:** shortest pauses in a bar of music.
24–25.   **first house:** highest rank. **first and second cause:** dueling terms
("first," offense is taken; "second," a challenge is given).
26.   **passado:** lunge. **punto reverso:** backhand stroke. **hay:** home thrust.

Mercutio. The pox of° such antic, lisping, affecting
fantasticoes°—these new tuners of accent! "By Jesu,
a very good blade! A very tall° man! A very good   30
whore!" Why, is not this a lamentable thing, grand
sir, that we should be thus afflicted with these
strange flies, these fashionmongers, these pardon-
me's, who stand so much on the new form° that
they cannot sit at ease on the old bench? O, their   35
bones,° their bones!

Enter ROMEO.

Benvolio. Here comes Romeo! Here comes Romeo!
Mercutio. Without his roe,° like a dried herring. O
flesh, flesh, how art thou fishified! Now is he for the
numbers° that Petrarch flowed in. Laura, to his lady,   40
was a kitchen wench (marry, she had a better love to
berhyme her), Dido° a dowdy, Cleopatra a gypsy, Helen
and Hero hildings° and harlots, Thisbe a gray
eye° or so, but not to the purpose. Signior Romeo,
bonjour! There's a French salutation to your French   45
slop.° You gave us the counterfeit° fairly last night.
Romeo. Good morrow to you both. What counterfeit did
I give you?

---

28.   **pox of:** plague on (curse on).
29.   **fantasticoes:** dandies; men who copy French manners and fashions.
30.   **tall:** brave.
34.   **new form:** new fashions.
36.   **bones:** pun on their use of the French *bon* ("good").
38.   **roe:** pun on *roe*, which means "female deer." *Roe* also means "fish eggs,"
      so Mercutio is also suggesting that love has made Romeo "gutless."
40.   **numbers:** verses. Petrarch was an Italian poet who wrote verses to a
      woman named Laura.
42.   **Dido:** in the *Aeneid,* queen of Carthage who loved Aeneas. (The
      women who follow also were famous lovers in literature: Cleopatra
      was the queen of Egypt loved by Antony; Helen of Troy was loved by
      Paris; Hero was loved by Leander; Thisbe was loved by Pyramus.)
43.   **hildings:** worthless ones.
43–44. **gray eye:** gleam in the eye.
46.   **slop:** loose trousers then popular in France. **counterfeit:** slip.

Mercutio. The slip, sir, the slip. Can you not conceive?° 50

Romeo. Pardon, good Mercutio. My business was great, and in such a case as mine a man may strain courtesy.

Mercutio. That's as much as to say, such a case° as yours constrains a man to bow in the hams.

Romeo. Meaning, to curtsy. 55

Mercutio. Thou hast most kindly hit it.

Romeo. A most courteous exposition.

Mercutio. Nay, I am the very pink of courtesy.

Romeo. Pink for flower.

Mercutio. Right. 60

Romeo. Why, then is my pump° well-flowered.°

Mercutio. Sure wit, follow me this jest now till thou hast worn out thy pump, that, when the single sole of it is worn, the jest may remain, after the wearing, solely singular. 65

Romeo. O single-soled jest, solely singular for the singleness!°

Mercutio. Come between us, good Benvolio! My wits faint.

Romeo. Swits° and spurs, swits and spurs; or I'll cry a match. 70

Mercutio. Nay, if our wits run the wild-goose chase, I am done; for thou hast more of the wild goose in one of thy wits than, I am sure, I have in my whole five. Was I with you there for the goose?° 75

Romeo. Thou wast never with me for anything when thou wast not there for the goose.°

Mercutio. I will bite thee by the ear for that jest.

---

50. **conceive:** understand.
53. **case:** set of clothes.
61. **pump:** shoe. **well-flowered:** pun on *well-floored.* Men's shoes were "pinked," or cut with decorations.
67. **singleness:** pun on *silliness.*
70. **Swits:** switches (a pun on *wits*).
74–75. **Was . . . goose?:** Was I right in calling you a goose?
77. **goose:** here, a woman.

Romeo. Nay, good goose, bite not!

Mercutio. Thy wit is a very bitter sweeting;° it is a most   80
sharp sauce.

Romeo. And is it not, then, well served in to a sweet
goose?°

Mercutio. O, here's a wit of cheveril,° that stretches from
an inch narrow to an ell broad!°   85

Romeo. I stretch it out for that word "broad," which,
added to the goose, proves thee far and wide a
broad° goose.

Mercutio. Why, is not this better now than groaning
for love? Now art thou sociable, now art thou Romeo;   90
now art thou what thou art, by art as well as by
nature. For this driveling love is like a great natu-
ral° that runs lolling up and down to hide his bauble°
in a hole.

Benvolio. Stop there, stop there!   95

Mercutio. Thou desirest me to stop in my tale against the
hair.°

Benvolio. Thou wouldst else have made thy tale large.°

Mercutio. O, thou art deceived! I would have made it
short; for I was come to the whole depth of my tale,   100
and meant indeed to occupy the argument no longer.

Romeo. Here's goodly gear!°

Enter NURSE *and her man* PETER.

A sail, a sail!

Mercutio. Two, two! A shirt and a smock.°

Nurse. Peter!   105

---

80. **bitter sweeting:** apple.
82–83. **sweet goose:** Sour sauce was considered best for sweet meat.
84. **cheveril:** kidskin (another reference to fashion).
85. **ell broad:** forty-five inches across.
88. **broad:** indecent.
93. **natural:** fool. **bauble:** literally, trinket or cheap jewel.
96–97. **against the hair:** against my better judgment.
98. **large:** indecent.
102. **gear:** matter for play and teasing.
104. **A shirt and a smock:** a man (shirt) and a woman (smock).

333333

333

Peter. Anon.

Nurse. My fan, Peter.

Mercutio. Good Peter, to hide her face; for her fan's the fairer face.

Nurse. God ye good morrow, gentlemen. 110

Mercutio. God ye good-den,° fair gentlewoman.

Nurse. Is it good-den?

Mercutio. 'Tis no less, I tell ye; for the bawdy hand of the dial is now upon the prick of noon.

Nurse. Out upon you! What a man are you! 115

Romeo. One, gentlewoman, that God hath made, himself to mar.

Nurse. By my troth, it is well said. "For himself to mar," quoth 'a? Gentlemen, can any of you tell me where I may find the young Romeo? 120

Romeo. I can tell you; but young Romeo will be older when you have found him than he was when you sought him. I am the youngest of that name, for fault of a worse.°

Nurse. You say well. 125

Mercutio. Yea, is the worst well? Very well took, i' faith! Wisely, wisely.

Nurse. If you be he, sir, I desire some confidence with you.

Benvolio. She will endite° him to some supper. 130

Mercutio. A bawd, a bawd, a bawd! So ho!

Romeo. What hast thou found?

Mercutio. No hare,° sir; unless a hare, sir, in a Lenten pie,° that is something stale and hoar° ere it be spent. 135

---

111. **God ye good-den:** God grant you a good evening.
123–124. **for fault of a worse:** for want of a better.
130. **endite:** invite. Benvolio mocks the nurse for saying "confidence" when she meant "conference."
133. **hare:** slang for "morally loose woman."
134. **Lenten pie:** rabbit pie, eaten sparingly during Lent, so that it is around for a long time and gets stale. **hoar:** gray with mold (the old nurse has gray hair).

He walks by them and sings.

> An old hare hoar,
> And an old hare hoar,
> Is very good meat in Lent;
> But a hare that is hoar
> Is too much for a score   140
> When it hoars ere it be spent.

Romeo, will you come to your father's? We'll to dinner thither.

Romeo. I will follow you.

Mercutio. Farewell, ancient lady. Farewell [*singing*]   145
"Lady, lady, lady."   [*Exeunt* MERCUTIO, BENVOLIO.]

Nurse. I pray you, sir, what saucy merchant was this that was so full of his ropery?°

Romeo. A gentleman, nurse, that loves to hear himself talk and will speak more in a minute than he will stand   150
to in a month.

Nurse. And 'a speak anything against me, I'll take him down, and 'a were lustier than he is, and twenty such Jacks; and if I cannot, I'll find those that shall. Scurvy knave! I am none of his flirt-gills;°   155
I am none of his skainsmates.° And thou must stand by too, and suffer every knave to use me at his pleasure!

Peter. I saw no man use you at his pleasure. If I had, my weapon should quickly have been out, I warrant   160
you. I dare draw as soon as another man, if I see occasion in a good quarrel, and the law on my side.

Nurse. Now, afore God, I am so vexed that every part about me quivers. Scurvy knave! Pray you, sir, a word; and, as I told you, my young lady bid me inquire   165
you out. What she bid me say, I will keep to myself; but first let me tell ye, if ye should lead her in a

---

148. **ropery:** The nurse means "roguery," or vulgar ways.
155. **flirt-gills:** flirty girls.
156. **skainsmates:** loose women.

fool's paradise, as they say, it were a very gross kind of
behavior, as they say; for the gentlewoman is young;
and therefore, if you should deal double with her,   170
truly it were an ill thing to be offered to any
gentlewoman, and very weak dealing.

Romeo. Nurse, commend me to thy lady and mistress. I
protest unto thee——

Nurse. Good heart, and i' faith I will tell her as much.   175
Lord, Lord, she will be a joyful woman.

Romeo. What wilt thou tell her, nurse? Thou dost not
mark° me.

Nurse. I will tell her, sir, that you do protest, which, as I
take it, is a gentlemanlike offer.   180

Romeo.
Bid her devise
Some means to come to shrift this afternoon;
And there she shall at Friar Laurence' cell
Be shrived° and married. Here is for thy pains.

Nurse. No, truly, sir; not a penny.   185

Romeo. Go to! I say you shall.

Nurse. This afternoon, sir? Well, she shall be there.

Romeo.
And stay, good nurse, behind the abbey wall.
Within this hour my man shall be with thee
And bring thee cords made like a tackled stair,°   190
Which to the high topgallant° of my joy
Must be my convoy° in the secret night.
Farewell. Be trusty, and I'll quit° thy pains.
Farewell. Commend me to thy mistress.

Nurse.
Now God in heaven bless thee! Hark you, sir.   195

---

178. **mark:** listen to.
184. **shrived:** forgiven of her sins.
190. **tackled stair:** rope ladder.
191. **topgallant:** highest platform on a sailing ship's mast.
192. **convoy:** means of conveyance.
193. **quit:** repay.

Romeo.
What say'st thou, my dear nurse?
Nurse.
Is your man secret? Did you ne'er hear say,
Two may keep counsel, putting one away?
Romeo.
Warrant thee my man's as true as steel.
Nurse. Well, sir, my mistress is the sweetest lady.   200
Lord, Lord! When 'twas a little prating thing—O,
there is a nobleman in town, one Paris, that would
fain lay knife aboard;° but she, good soul, had as
lieve see a toad, a very toad, as see him. I anger her
sometimes, and tell her that Paris is the prop-   205
erer man; but I'll warrant you, when I say so, she
looks as pale as any clout° in the versal° world. Doth
not rosemary and Romeo begin both with a
letter?
Romeo. Ay, nurse; what of that? Both with an R.   210
Nurse. Ah, mocker! That's the dog's name.° R is for
the—no; I know it begins with some other letter;
and she hath the prettiest sententious° of it, of
you and rosemary, that it would do you good to
hear it.   215
Romeo. Commend me to thy lady.
Nurse. Ay, a thousand times. [*Exit* ROMEO.] Peter!
Peter. Anon.
Nurse. Before, and apace.   [*Exit after* PETER.]

Scene 5. *Capulet's orchard.*

Enter JULIET.

Juliet.
The clock struck nine when I did send the nurse;

---

203. **lay knife aboard:** take a slice (lay claim to Juliet).
207. **clout:** rag. **versal:** universal.
211. In other words, a dog's growl has an "r" sound ("r-r-r-r").
213. **sententious:** The nurse means "sentence."

In half an hour she promised to return.
Perchance she cannot meet him. That's not so.
O, she is lame! Love's heralds should be thoughts,
Which ten times faster glide than the sun's beams   5
Driving back shadows over low'ring hills.   ✦
Therefore do nimble-pinioned doves° draw Love,
And therefore hath the wind-swift Cupid wings.
Now is the sun upon the highmost hill
Of this day's journey, and from nine till twelve   10
Is three long hours; yet she is not come.
Had she affections and warm youthful blood,
She would be as swift in motion as a ball;
My words would bandy her° to my sweet love,
And his to me.   15
But old folks, many feign as they were dead—
Unwieldy, slow, heavy, and pale as lead.

Enter NURSE *and* PETER.

O God, she comes! O honey nurse, what news?
Hast thou met with him? Send thy man away.
Nurse.
Peter, stay at the gate.   [*Exit* PETER.]   20
Juliet.
Now, good sweet nurse—O Lord, why look'st thou
    sad?
Though news be sad, yet tell them merrily;
If good, thou sham'st the music of sweet news
By playing it to me with so sour a face.
Nurse.
I am aweary, give me leave awhile.   25
Fie, how my bones ache! What a jaunce° have I!

II.5.7. nimble-pinioned doves: Nimble-winged doves were said to pull
    the chariot of Venus, the goddess of love.
14.   bandy her: send her back and forth, like a tennis ball.
26.   jaunce: tiring journey.

Juliet.
> I would thou hadst my bones, and I thy news.
> Nay, come, I pray thee speak. Good, good nurse, speak.

Nurse.
> Jesu, what haste! Can you not stay° awhile?
> Do you not see that I am out of breath?   30

Juliet.
> How art thou out of breath when thou hast breath
> To say to me that thou art out of breath?
> The excuse that thou dost make in this delay
> Is longer than the tale thou dost excuse.
> Is thy news good or bad? Answer to that.   35
> Say either, and I'll stay the circumstance.°
> Let me be satisfied, is't good or bad?

Nurse. Well, you have made a simple° choice; you know
> not how to choose a man. Romeo? No, not he. Though
> his face be better than any man's, yet his leg excels   40
> all men's; and for a hand and a foot, and a body,
> though they be not to be talked on, yet they are past
> compare. He is not the flower of courtesy, but, I'll
> warrant him, as gentle as a lamb. Go thy ways,
> wench; serve God. What, have you dined at home?   45

Juliet.
> No, no. But all this did I know before.
> What says he of our marriage? What of that?

Nurse.
> Lord, how my head aches! What a head have I!
> It beats as it would fall in twenty pieces.
> My back a'° t' other side—ah, my back, my back!   50
> Beshrew° your heart for sending me about
> To catch my death with jauncing up and down!

---

29. **stay:** wait.
36. **stay the circumstance:** wait for the details.
38. **simple:** foolish.
50. **a':** on.
51. **Beshrew:** shame on.

Juliet.
 I' faith, I am sorry that thou art not well.
 Sweet, sweet, sweet nurse, tell me, what says my love?
Nurse. Your love says, like an honest gentleman, and   55
 a courteous, and a kind, and a handsome, and, I
 warrant, a virtuous—where is your mother?
Juliet.
 Where is my mother? Why, she is within.
 Where should she be? How oddly thou repliest!
 "Your love says, like an honest gentleman,   60
 'Where is your mother?' "
Nurse.   O God's Lady dear!
 Are you so hot?° Marry come up, I trow.°
 Is this the poultice for my aching bones?
 Henceforward do your messages yourself.
Juliet.
 Here's such a coil!° Come, what says Romeo?   65
Nurse.
 Have you got leave to go to shrift today?
Juliet.
 I have.
Nurse.
 Then hie you hence to Friar Laurence' cell;
 There stays a husband to make you a wife.
 Now comes the wanton blood up in your cheeks.   70
 They'll be in scarlet straight at any news.
 Hie you to church; I must another way,
 To fetch a ladder, by the which your love
 Must climb a bird's nest soon when it is dark.
 I am the drudge, and toil in your delight;   75
 But you shall bear the burden soon at night.
 Go; I'll to dinner; hie you to the cell.
Juliet.
 Hie to high fortune! Honest nurse, farewell. [*Exeunt.*]

---

 62. hot: angry. **Marry come up, I trow:** something like, "By the Virgin
   Mary, come off it, I swear."
 65. coil: fuss.

Scene 6. *Friar Laurence's cell.*

Enter FRIAR LAURENCE *and* ROMEO.

Friar.
 So smile the heavens upon this holy act
 That afterhours with sorrow chide us not!
Romeo.
 Amen, amen! But come what sorrow can,
 It cannot countervail° the exchange of joy
 That one short minute gives me in her sight.   5
 Do thou but close our hands with holy words,
 Then love-devouring death do what he dare—
 It is enough I may but call her mine.
Friar.
 These violent delights have violent ends
 And in their triumph die, like fire and powder,°   10
 Which, as they kiss, consume. The sweetest honey
 Is loathsome in his own deliciousness
 And in the taste confounds° the appetite.
 Therefore love moderately: long love doth so;
 Too swift arrives as tardy as too slow.   15

Enter JULIET.

 Here comes the lady. O, so light a foot
 Will ne'er wear out the everlasting flint.°
 A lover may bestride the gossamers°
 That idle in the wanton summer air,
 And yet not fall; so light is vanity.°   20
Juliet.
 Good even to my ghostly confessor.

II.6.4. **countervail:** match or equal.
10. **powder:** gunpowder.
13. **confounds:** destroys.
17. **flint:** stone.
18. **gossamers:** finest spider threads.
20. **vanity:** fleeting human love.

Friar.
Romeo shall thank thee, daughter, for us both.
Juliet.
As much to him,° else is his thanks too much.
Romeo.
Ah, Juliet, if the measure of thy joy
Be heaped like mine, and that thy skill be more   25
To blazon° it, then sweeten with thy breath
This neighbor air, and let rich music's tongue
Unfold the imagined happiness that both
Receive in either by this dear encounter.
Juliet.
Conceit,° more rich in matter than in words,   30
Brags of his substance, not of ornament.°
They are but beggars that can count their worth;
But my true love is grown to such excess
I cannot sum up sum of half my wealth.
Friar.
Come, come with me, and we will make short work;   35
For, by your leaves, you shall not stay alone
Till holy church incorporate two in one.   [*Exeunt.*]

---

23. As much to him: the same to him.
26. blazon: describe.
30. Conceit: genuine understanding.
31. ornament: fancy language.

Act III

Scene 1. *A public place.*

Enter MERCUTIO, BENVOLIO, *and* MEN.

Benvolio.

I pray thee, good Mercutio, let's retire.
The day is hot, the Capels° are abroad,
And, if we meet, we shall not 'scape a brawl,
For now, these hot days, is the mad blood stirring.

Mercutio. Thou art like one of these fellows that,   5
when he enters the confines of a tavern, claps me
his sword upon the table and says, "God send me no
need of thee!" and by the operation of the second
cup draws him on the drawer,° when indeed there is
no need.   10

Benvolio. Am I like such a fellow?

Mercutio. Come, come, thou art as hot a Jack in thy
mood as any in Italy; and as soon moved to be moody,
and as soon moody to be moved.

Benvolio. And what to?   15

Mercutio. Nay, and there were two such, we should have
none shortly, for one would kill the other. Thou!
Why, thou wilt quarrel with a man that hath a hair
more or a hair less in his beard than thou hast.
Thou wilt quarrel with a man for cracking nuts, hav-   20
ing no other reason but because thou hast hazel
eyes. What eye but such an eye would spy out such a
quarrel? Thy head is as full of quarrels as an egg
is full of meat; and yet thy head hath been beaten

III.1.2. **Capels:** Capulets.
9.   **draws him on the drawer:** draws his sword on the waiter (who
        "draws" the drink).
74

as addle° as an egg for quarreling. Thou hast quar-   25
reled with a man for coughing in the street, because
he hath wakened thy dog that hath lain asleep in the
sun. Didst thou not fall out with a tailor for wearing his new doublet° before Easter? With another
for tying his new shoes with old riband? And yet   30
thou wilt tutor me from quarreling!
Benvolio. And I were so apt to quarrel as thou art, any
man should buy the fee simple of° my life for an
hour and a quarter.
Mercutio. The fee simple? O simple!°   35

Enter TYBALT *and others.*

Benvolio. By my head, here come the Capulets.
Mercutio. By my heel, I care not.
Tybalt.
Follow me close, for I will speak to them.
Gentlemen, good-den. A word with one of you.
Mercutio.
And but one word with one of us?   40
Couple it with something; make it a word and a blow.
Tybalt. You shall find me apt enough to that, sir, and you
will give me occasion.
Mercutio. Could you not take some occasion without
giving?   45
Tybalt. Mercutio, thou consortest with Romeo.
Mercutio. Consort?° What, dost thou make us minstrels?
And thou make minstrels of us, look to hear nothing
but discords. Here's my fiddlestick;° here's that shall
make you dance. Zounds,° consort!   50

25. **addle:** rotten.
29. **doublet:** short, close-fitting jacket.
33. **buy the fee simple of:** buy insurance on.
35. **O simple!:** O fool!
47. **Consort:** Mercutio pretends to think that Tybalt means a *consort*, or group of musicians.
49. **fiddlestick:** bow for playing violin-like instrument (referring to his sword).
50. **Zounds:** slang for "by God's wounds."

Benvolio.
We talk here in the public haunt of men.
Either withdraw unto some private place,
Or reason coldly of your grievances,
Or else depart. Here all eyes gaze on us.
Mercutio.
Men's eyes were made to look, and let them gaze.　　55
I will not budge for no man's pleasure, I.

Enter ROMEO.

Tybalt.
Well, peace be with you, sir. Here comes my man.
Mercutio.
But I'll be hanged, sir, if he wear your livery.°
Marry, go before to field,° he'll be your follower!
Your worship in that sense may call him man.　　60
Tybalt.
Romeo, the love I bear thee can afford
No better term than this: thou art a villain.°
Romeo.
Tybalt, the reason that I have to love thee
Doth much excuse the appertaining° rage
To such a greeting. Villain am I none.　　65
Therefore farewell. I see thou knowest me not.
Tybalt.
Boy, this shall not excuse the injuries
That thou hast done me; therefore turn and draw.
Romeo.
I do protest I never injured thee,
But love thee better than thou canst devise°　　70
Till thou shalt know the reason of my love;

---

58. **livery:** servant's uniform. By *man*, Tybalt meant "target"; but
　　Mercutio uses the word to mean "servant."
59. **field:** dueling place.
62. **villain:** boor; clumsy, stupid fellow.
64. **appertaining:** understandable.
70. **devise:** guess.

And so, good Capulet, which name I tender°
As dearly as mine own, be satisfied.
Mercutio.
O calm, dishonorable, vile submission!
Alla stoccata° carries it away.   75

Draws.

Tybalt, you ratcatcher, will you walk?°
Tybalt.
What wouldst thou have with me?
Mercutio. Good King of Cats, nothing but one of your
nine lives. That I mean to make bold withal,° and,
as you shall use me hereafter, dry-beat° the rest of   80
the eight. Will you pluck your sword out of his
pilcher° by the ears? Make haste, lest mine be about
your ears ere it be out.
Tybalt. I am for you.

Draws.

Romeo.
Gentle Mercutio, put thy rapier up.   85
Mercutio. Come, sir, your passado!

They fight.

Romeo.
Draw, Benvolio; beat down their weapons.
Gentlemen, for shame! Forbear this outrage!
Tybalt, Mercutio, the prince expressly hath
Forbid this bandying° in Verona streets.   90
Hold, Tybalt! Good Mercutio!

---

72. **tender:** treasure.
75. **Alla stoccata:** "at the thrust," a fencing term.
76. **walk:** make a move.
79. **make bold withal:** make free with (take away).
80. **dry-beat:** beat soundly.
82. **pilcher:** scabbard (sword holder).
90. **bandying:** fighting.

TYBALT *under Romeo's arm thrusts* MERCUTIO *in, and flies.*

Mercutio.   I am hurt.
A plague a' both houses! I am sped.°
Is he gone and hath nothing?
Benvolio.   What, art thou hurt?
Mercutio.
Ay, ay, a scratch, a scratch. Marry, 'tis enough.
Where is my page? Go, villain, fetch a surgeon.   95

                              Exit PAGE.

Romeo.
Courage, man. The hurt cannot be much.
Mercutio. No, 'tis not so deep as a well, nor so wide
as a church door; but 'tis enough, 'twill serve. Ask
for me tomorrow, and you shall find me a grave man.
I am peppered,° I warrant, for this world. A plague   100
a' both your houses! Zounds, a dog, a rat, a mouse,
a cat, to scratch a man to death! A braggart, a rogue,
a villain, that fights by the book of arithmetic!° Why
the devil came you between us? I was hurt under
your arm.   105
Romeo.
I thought all for the best.
Mercutio.
Help me into some house, Benvolio,
Or I shall faint. A plague a' both your houses!
They have made worms' meat of me. I have it,
And soundly too. Your houses!   110

                Exeunt MERCUTIO *and* BENVOLIO.

---

92. **sped:** destroyed; done for.
100. **peppered:** given a deadly wound ("peppered" food is ready to eat;
      Mercutio is "ready" to die).
103. **fights by the book of arithmetic:** fights according to formal rules for
      fencing.

Romeo.

This gentleman, the prince's near ally,°
My very friend, hath got this mortal hurt
In my behalf—my reputation stained
With Tybalt's slander—Tybalt, that an hour
Hath been my cousin. O sweet Juliet,   115
Thy beauty hath made me effeminate
And in my temper soft'ned valor's steel!

Enter BENVOLIO.

Benvolio.

O Romeo, Romeo, brave Mercutio is dead!
That gallant spirit hath aspired° the clouds,
Which too untimely here did scorn the earth.   120

Romeo.

This day's black fate on more days doth depend;°
This but begins the woe others must end.

Enter TYBALT.

Benvolio.

Here comes the furious Tybalt back again.

Romeo.

Alive in triumph, and Mercutio slain?
Away to heaven respective lenity,   125
And fire-eyed fury be my conduct now!
Now, Tybalt, take the "villain" back again
That late thou gavest me; for Mercutio's soul
Is but a little way above our heads,
Staying for thine to keep him company.   130
Either thou or I, or both, must go with him.

Tybalt.

Thou, wretched boy, that didst consort him here,
Shalt with him hence.

---

111. **ally:** relative. Mercutio was related to Verona's Prince Escalus.
119. **aspired:** soared to.
121. **depend:** hang over.

Romeo. This shall determine that.

They fight. TYBALT *falls.*

Benvolio.
Romeo, away, be gone!
The citizens are up, and Tybalt slain.   135
Stand not amazed. The prince will doom thee death
If thou art taken. Hence, be gone, away!
Romeo.
O, I am fortune's fool!
Benvolio. Why dost thou stay?

Exit ROMEO.

Enter CITIZENS.

Citizen.
Which way ran he that killed Mercutio?
Tybalt, that murderer, which way ran he?   140
Benvolio.
There lies that Tybalt.
Citizen. Up, sir, go with me.
I charge thee in the prince's name obey.

Enter PRINCE, *old* MONTAGUE, CAPULET, *their* WIVES, *and all.*

Prince.
Where are the vile beginners of this fray?
Benvolio.
O noble prince, I can discover° all
The unlucky manage° of this fatal brawl.   145
There lies the man, slain by young Romeo,
That slew thy kinsman, brave Mercutio.
Lady Capulet.
Tybalt, my cousin! O my brother's child!
O prince! O cousin! Husband! O, the blood is spilled
Of my dear kinsman! Prince, as thou art true,   150

---

144. **discover:** tell.
145. **manage:** circumstances.

For blood of ours shed blood of Montague.
O cousin, cousin!
Prince.
Benvolio, who began this bloody fray?
Benvolio.
Tybalt, here slain, whom Romeo's hand did slay.
Romeo, that spoke him fair, bid him bethink   155
How nice° the quarrel was, and urged° withal
Your high displeasure. All this—utterèd
With gentle breath, calm look, knees humbly bowed—
Could not take truce with the unruly spleen°
Of Tybalt deaf to peace, but that he tilts°   160
With piercing steel at bold Mercutio's breast;
Who, all as hot, turns deadly point to point,
And, with a martial scorn, with one hand beats
Cold death aside and with the other sends
It back to Tybalt, whose dexterity   165
Retorts it. Romeo he cries aloud,
"Hold, friends! Friends, part!" and swifter than his
     tongue,
His agile arm beats down their fatal points,
And 'twixt them rushes; underneath whose arm
An envious° thrust from Tybalt hit the life   170
Of stout Mercutio, and then Tybalt fled;
But by and by comes back to Romeo,
Who had but newly entertained° revenge,
And to't they go like lightning; for, ere I
Could draw to part them, was stout Tybalt slain;   175
And, as he fell, did Romeo turn and fly.
This is the truth, or let Benvolio die.
Lady Capulet.
He is a kinsman to the Montague;
Affection makes him false, he speaks not true.

---

156. **nice:** petty; trifling. **urged:** mentioned.
159. **spleen:** anger.
160. **tilts:** thrusts.
170. **envious:** full of hatred.
173. **entertained:** thought of.

Some twenty of them fought in this black strife,   180
And all those twenty could but kill one life.
I beg for justice, which thou, prince, must give.
Romeo slew Tybalt; Romeo must not live.
Prince.
Romeo slew him; he slew Mercutio.
Who now the price of his dear blood doth owe?   185
Montague.
⸱ Not Romeo, prince; he was Mercutio's friend;
His fault concludes but what the law should end,
The life of Tybalt.
Prince.   And for that offense
Immediately we do exile him hence.
I have an interest in your hate's proceeding,   190
My blood° for your rude brawls doth lie a-bleeding;
But I'll amerce° you with so strong a fine
That you shall all repent the loss of mine.
I will be deaf to pleading and excuses;
Nor tears nor prayers shall purchase out abuses.   195
Therefore use none. Let Romeo hence in haste,
Else, when he is found, that hour is his last.
Bear hence this body and attend our will.
Mercy but murders, pardoning those that kill.

Exit with others.

Scene 2. *Capulet's orchard.*

Enter JULIET *alone.*

Juliet.
Gallop apace, you fiery-footed steeds,°
Towards Phoebus' lodging! Such a wagoner

---

191. My blood: that is, Mercutio, his blood relative.
192. amerce: punish.
III.2.1. steeds: horses (that pull the sun god Phoebus's chariot across the
  sky each day).

As Phaethon° would whip you to the west
And bring in cloudy night immediately.
Spread thy close curtain, love-performing night,   5
That runaways' eyes may wink,° and Romeo
Leap to these arms untalked of and unseen.
Lovers can see to do their amorous rites,
And by their own beauties; or, if love be blind,
It best agrees with night. Come, civil° night,   10
Thou sober-suited matron all in black,
And learn me how to lose a winning match,
Played for a pair of stainless maidenhoods.
Hood° my unmanned° blood, bating° in my cheeks,
With thy black mantle till strange° love grow bold,   15
Think true love acted simple modesty.
Come, night; come, Romeo; come, thou day in night;
For thou wilt lie upon the wings of night
Whiter than new snow upon a raven's back.
Come, gentle night; come, loving, black-browed night;   20
Give me my Romeo; and, when he shall die,
Take him and cut him out in little stars,
And he will make the face of heaven so fine
That all the world will be in love with night
And pay no worship to the garish sun.   25
O, I have bought the mansion of a love,
But not possessed it; and though I am sold,
Not yet enjoyed. So tedious is this day
As is the night before some festival
To an impatient child that hath new robes   30
And may not wear them. O, here comes my nurse,

Enter NURSE, *with a ladder of cords.*

And she brings news; and every tongue that speaks

---

3. **Phaethon:** Phoebus's reckless son, who couldn't hold the horses.
6. **That runaways' eyes may wink:** so that the eyes of the sun god's horses may shut.
10. **civil:** well-behaved.
14. **Hood:** cover. **unmanned:** unmated. **bating:** fluttering.
15. **strange:** unfamiliar.

But Romeo's name speaks heavenly eloquence.
Now, nurse, what news? What hast thou there, the
   cords
That Romeo bid thee fetch?

Nurse.   Ay, ay, the cords.   35
Juliet.
  Ay me! What news? Why dost thou wring thy hands?
Nurse.
  Ah, weraday!° He's dead, he's dead, he's dead!
  We are undone, lady, we are undone!
  Alack the day! He's gone, he's killed, he's dead!
Juliet.
  Can heaven be so envious?
Nurse.   Romeo can,   40
  Though heaven cannot. O Romeo, Romeo!
  Who ever would have thought it? Romeo!
Juliet.
  What devil art thou that dost torment me thus?
  This torture should be roared in dismal hell.
  Hath Romeo slain himself? Say thou but "Ay,"   45
  And that bare vowel "I" shall poison more
  Than the death-darting eye of cockatrice.°
  I am not I, if there be such an "Ay,"
  Or those eyes' shot that make thee answer "Ay."
  If he be slain, say "Ay"; or if not, "No."   50
  Brief sounds determine of my weal or woe.
Nurse.
  I saw the wound, I saw it with mine eyes,
  (God save the mark!)° here on his manly breast.
  A piteous corse,° a bloody piteous corse;
  Pale, pale as ashes, all bedaubed in blood,   55
  All in gore-blood. I swounded° at the sight.

---

37. **weraday!:** well-a-day! (or alas!)
47. **cockatrice:** legendary serpent that could kill by a glance.
53. **God save the mark!:** God forbid!
54. **corse:** corpse.
56. **swounded:** fainted.

Juliet.
    O, break, my heart! Poor bankrout,° break at once!
    To prison, eyes; ne'er look on liberty!
    Vile earth,° to earth resign; end motion here,
    And thou and Romeo press one heavy bier!   60
Nurse.
    O Tybalt, Tybalt, the best friend I had!
    O courteous Tybalt! Honest gentleman!
    That ever I should live to see thee dead!
Juliet.
    What storm is this that blows so contrary?
    Is Romeo slaught'red, and is Tybalt dead?   65
    My dearest cousin, and my dearer lord?
    Then, dreadful trumpet, sound the general doom!
    For who is living, if those two are gone?
Nurse.
    Tybalt is gone, and Romeo banishèd;
    Romeo that killed him, he is banishèd.   70
Juliet.
    O God! Did Romeo's hand shed Tybalt's blood?
Nurse.
    It did, it did! Alas the day, it did!
Juliet.
    O serpent heart, hid with a flow'ring face!
    Did ever dragon keep so fair a cave?
    Beautiful tyrant! Fiend angelical!   75
    Dove-feathered raven! Wolvish-ravening lamb!
    Despisèd substance of divinest show!
    Just opposite to what thou justly seem'st—
    A damnèd saint, an honorable villain!
    O nature, what hadst thou to do in hell   80
    When thou didst bower the spirit of a fiend
    In mortal paradise of such sweet flesh?
    Was ever book containing such vile matter

---

57. **bankrout:** bankrupt.
59. **Vile earth:** Juliet refers to herself.

So fairly bound? O, that deceit should dwell
In such a gorgeous palace!
Nurse.   There's no trust,   85
No faith, no honesty in men; all perjured,
All forsworn, all naught, all dissemblers.°
Ah, where's my man? Give me some aqua vitae.°
These griefs, these woes, these sorrows make me old.
Shame come to Romeo!
Juliet.   Blistered be thy tongue   90
For such a wish! He was not born to shame.
Upon his brow shame is ashamed to sit;
For 'tis a throne where honor may be crowned
Sole monarch of the universal earth.
O, what a beast was I to chide at him!   95
Nurse.
Will you speak well of him that killed your cousin?
Juliet.
Shall I speak ill of him that is my husband?
Ah, poor my lord, what tongue shall smooth thy name
When I, thy three-hours wife, have mangled it?
But wherefore, villain, didst thou kill my cousin?   100
That villain cousin would have killed my husband.
Back, foolish tears, back to your native spring!
Your tributary drops° belong to woe,
Which you, mistaking, offer up to joy.
My husband lives, that Tybalt would have slain;   105
And Tybalt's dead, that would have slain my husband.
All this is comfort; wherefore weep I then?
Some word there was, worser than Tybalt's death,
That murd'red me. I would forget it fain;°
But O, it presses to my memory   110
Like damnèd guilty deeds to sinners' minds!
"Tybalt is dead, and Romeo—banishèd."

---

87. **dissemblers:** liars.
88. **aqua vitae:** brandy (Latin for "water of life").
103. **tributary drops:** tears poured out in tribute.
109. **fain:** willingly.

That "banishèd," that one word "banishèd,"
Hath slain ten thousand Tybalts. Tybalt's death
Was woe enough, if it had ended there;   115
Or, if sour woe delights in fellowship
And needly will be ranked with° other griefs,
Why followed not, when she said "Tybalt's dead,"
Thy father, or thy mother, nay, or both,
Which modern° lamentation might have moved?°   120
But with a rearward° following Tybalt's death,
"Romeo is banishèd"—to speak that word
Is father, mother, Tybalt, Romeo, Juliet,
All slain, all dead. "Romeo is banishèd"—
There is no end, no limit, measure, bound,   125
In that word's death; no words can that woe sound.
Where is my father and my mother, nurse?

Nurse.
Weeping and wailing over Tybalt's corse.
Will you go to them? I will bring you thither.

Juliet.
Wash they his wounds with tears? Mine shall be spent,   130
When theirs are dry, for Romeo's banishment.
Take up those cords. Poor ropes, you are beguiled,
Both you and I, for Romeo is exiled.
He made you for a highway to my bed;
But I, a maid, die maiden-widowèd.   135
Come, cords; come, nurse. I'll to my wedding bed;
And death, not Romeo, take my maidenhead!

Nurse.
Hie to your chamber. I'll find Romeo
To comfort you. I wot° well where he is.
Hark ye, your Romeo will be here at night.   140
I'll to him; he is hid at Laurence' cell.

---

117. **ranked with:** accompanied by.
120. **modern:** normal. **moved:** provoked.
121. **rearward:** soldiers at the rear of a troop; here, an additional source of
    injury and pain after the bad news about Tybalt.
139. **wot:** know.

Juliet.

O, find him! Give this ring to my true knight
And bid him come to take his last farewell.

Exit with NURSE.

Scene 3. *Friar Laurence's cell.*

Enter FRIAR LAURENCE.

Friar.

Romeo, come forth; come forth, thou fearful man.
Affliction is enamored of thy parts,
And thou art wedded to calamity.

Enter ROMEO.

Romeo.

Father, what news? What is the prince's doom?
What sorrow craves acquaintance at my hand   5
That I yet know not?
Friar.   Too familiar
Is my dear son with such sour company.
I bring thee tidings of the prince's doom.
Romeo.
What less than doomsday° is the prince's doom?
Friar.
A gentler judgment vanished° from his lips—   10
Not body's death, but body's banishment.
Romeo.
Ha, banishment? Be merciful, say "death";
For exile hath more terror in his look,
Much more than death. Do not say "banishment."

III.3.9. **doomsday:** my death.
10. vanished: came.

Friar.

    Here from Verona art thou banishèd.   15

    Be patient, for the world is broad and wide.

Romeo.

    There is no world without Verona walls,

    But purgatory, torture, hell itself.

    Hence banishèd is banished from the world,

    And world's exile is death. Then "banishèd"   20

    Is death mistermed. Calling death "banishèd,"

    Thou cut'st my head off with a golden ax

    And smilest upon the stroke that murders me.

Friar.

    O deadly sin! O rude unthankfulness!

    Thy fault our law calls death; but the kind prince,   25

    Taking thy part, hath rushed aside the law,

    And turned that black word "death" to "banishment."

    This is dear mercy, and thou see'st it not.

Romeo.

    'Tis torture, and not mercy. Heaven is here,

    Where Juliet lives; and every cat and dog   30

    And little mouse, every unworthy thing,

    Live here in heaven and may look on her;

    But Romeo may not. More validity,°

    More honorable state, more courtship lives

    In carrion flies than Romeo. They may seize   35

    On the white wonder of dear Juliet's hand

    And steal immortal blessing from her lips,

    Who, even in pure and vestal modesty,

    Still blush, as thinking their own kisses sin;

    But Romeo may not, he is banishèd.   40

    Flies may do this but I from this must fly;

    They are freemen, but I am banishèd.

    And sayest thou yet that exile is not death?

    Hadst thou no poison mixed, no sharp-ground knife,

    No sudden mean of death, though ne'er so mean,   45

---

33. **validity:** value.

But "banishèd" to kill me—"banishèd"?
O friar, the damnèd use that word in hell;
Howling attends it! How hast thou the heart,
Being a divine, a ghostly confessor,
A sin-absolver, and my friend professed,   50
To mangle me with that word "banishèd"?
Friar.
Thou fond° mad man, hear me a little speak.
Romeo.
O, thou wilt speak again of banishment.
Friar.
I'll give thee armor to keep off that word;
Adversity's sweet milk, philosophy,   55
To comfort thee, though thou art banishèd.
Romeo.
Yet "banishèd"? Hang up philosophy!
Unless philosophy can make a Juliet,
Displant a town, reverse a prince's doom,
It helps not, it prevails not. Talk no more.   60
Friar.
O, then I see that madmen have no ears.
Romeo.
How should they, when that wise men have no eyes?
Friar.
Let me dispute with thee of thy estate.°
Romeo.
Thou canst not speak of that thou dost not feel.
Wert thou as young as I, Juliet thy love,   65
An hour but married, Tybalt murderèd,
Doting like me, and like me banishèd,
Then mightst thou speak, then mightst thou tear thy
      hair,
And fall upon the ground, as I do now,
Taking the measure of an unmade grave.   70

---

52. **fond:** foolish.
63. **estate:** circumstances.

The NURSE *knocks.*

Friar.
Arise, one knocks. Good Romeo, hide thyself.
Romeo.
Not I; unless the breath of heartsick groans
Mistlike infold me from the search of eyes.

Knock.

Friar.
Hark, how they knock! Who's there? Romeo, arise;
Thou wilt be taken.—Stay awhile!—Stand up;   75

Knock.

Run to my study.—By and by!—God's will,
What simpleness is this.—I come, I come!

Knock.

Who knocks so hard? Whence come you? What's
    your will?

Enter NURSE.

Nurse.
Let me come in, and you shall know my errand.
I come from Lady Juliet.
Friar.   Welcome then.   80
Nurse.
O holy friar, O, tell me, holy friar,
Where is my lady's lord, where's Romeo?
Friar.
There on the ground, with his own tears made drunk.
Nurse.
O, he is even in my mistress' case,°
Just in her case! O woeful sympathy!   85
Piteous predicament! Even so lies she,

---

84. **case:** condition.

Blubb'ring and weeping, weeping and blubb'ring.
Stand up, stand up! Stand, and you be a man.
For Juliet's sake, for her sake, rise and stand!
Why should you fall into so deep an O?°   90
Romeo [*rises*]. Nurse——
Nurse.

    Ah sir, ah sir! Death's the end of all.
Romeo.

    Spakest thou of Juliet? How is it with her?
    Doth not she think me an old murderer,
    Now I have stained the childhood of our joy   95
    With blood removed but little from her own?
    Where is she? And how doth she? And what says
    My concealed lady to our canceled love?
Nurse.

    O, she says nothing, sir, but weeps and weeps;
    And now falls on her bed, and then starts up,   100
    And Tybalt calls; and then on Romeo cries,
    And then down falls again.
Romeo.   As if that name,
    Shot from the deadly level° of a gun,
    Did murder her; as that name's cursèd hand
    Murdered her kinsman. O, tell me, friar, tell me,   105
    In what vile part of this anatomy
    Doth my name lodge? Tell me, that I may sack°
    The hateful mansion.

He offers to stab himself, and NURSE *snatches the dagger away.*

Friar.   Hold thy desperate hand.
    Art thou a man? Thy form cries out thou art;
    Thy tears are womanish, thy wild acts denote   110
    The unreasonable fury of a beast.

---

  90. O: cry of grief.
  103. level: aim.
  107. sack: destroy.

Unseemly woman in a seeming man!
And ill-beseeming beast in seeming both!
Thou hast amazed me. By my holy order,
I thought thy disposition better tempered.   115
Hast thou slain Tybalt? Wilt thou slay thyself?
And slay thy lady that in thy life lives,
By doing damnèd hate upon thyself?
Why rail'st thou on thy birth, the heaven, and earth?
Since birth and heaven and earth,° all three do meet   120
In thee at once; which thou at once wouldst lose.
Fie, fie, thou sham'st thy shape, thy love, thy wit,
Which,° like a usurer, abound'st in all,
And usest none in that true use indeed
Which should bedeck° thy shape, thy love, thy wit.   125
Thy noble shape is but a form of wax,
Digressing from the valor of a man;
Thy dear love sworn but hollow perjury,
Killing that love which thou hast vowed to cherish;
Thy wit, that ornament to shape and love,   130
Misshapen in the conduct° of them both,
Like powder in a skill-less soldier's flask,
Is set afire by thine own ignorance,
And thou dismembered with thine own defense.°
What, rouse thee, man! Thy Juliet is alive,   135
For whose dear sake thou wast but lately dead.
There art thou happy.° Tybalt would kill thee,
But thou slewest Tybalt. There art thou happy.
The law, that threatened death, becomes thy friend
And turns it to exile. There art thou happy.   140
A pack of blessings light upon thy back;

---

120. birth and heaven and earth: family origin, soul, and body.
123. Which: who (speaking of Romeo).
125. bedeck: honor.
131. conduct: management.
134. And . . . defense: Romeo's own mind (wit), which should protect him, is destroying him.
137. happy: lucky.

Happiness courts thee in her best array;
But, like a misbehaved and sullen wench,
Thou pouts upon thy fortune and thy love.
Take heed, take heed, for such die miserable.   145
Go get thee to thy love, as was decreed,
Ascend her chamber, hence and comfort her.
But look thou stay not till the watch be set,
For then thou canst not pass to Mantua,
Where thou shalt live till we can find a time   150
To blaze° your marriage, reconcile your friends,
Beg pardon of the prince, and call thee back
With twenty hundred thousand times more joy
Than thou went'st forth in lamentation.
Go before, nurse. Commend me to thy lady,   155
And bid her hasten all the house to bed,
Which heavy sorrow makes them apt unto.
Romeo is coming.

Nurse.

O Lord, I could have stayed here all the night
To hear good counsel. O, what learning is!   160
My lord, I'll tell my lady you will come.

Romeo.

Do so, and bid my sweet prepare to chide.

NURSE *offers to go in and turns again.*

Nurse.

Here, sir, a ring she bid me give you, sir.
Hie you, make haste, for it grows very late.   [*Exit.*]

Romeo.

How well my comfort is revived by this!   165

Friar.

Go hence; good night; and here stands all your state:°
Either be gone before the watch be set,
Or by the break of day disguised from hence.

---

151. **blaze:** announce.
166. **state:** situation.

Sojourn in Mantua. I'll find out your man,
And he shall signify from time to time   170
Every good hap to you that chances here.
Give me thy hand. 'Tis late. Farewell; good night.
Romeo.
But that a joy past joy calls out on me,
It were a grief so brief to part with thee.
Farewell.   [*Exeunt.*]   175

Scene 4. *A room in Capulet's house.*

Enter old CAPULET, *his wife,* LADY CAPULET, *and* PARIS.

Capulet.
Things have fallen out, sir, so unluckily
That we have had no time to move° our daughter.
Look you, she loved her kinsman Tybalt dearly,
And so did I. Well, we were born to die.
'Tis very late; she'll not come down tonight.   5
I promise you, but for your company,
I would have been abed an hour ago.
Paris.
These times of woe afford no times to woo.
Madam, good night. Commend me to your daughter.
Lady Capulet.
I will, and know her mind early tomorrow;   10
Tonight she's mewed up to her heaviness.°
Capulet.
Sir Paris, I will make a desperate tender°
Of my child's love. I think she will be ruled
In all respects by me; nay more, I doubt it not.
Wife, go you to her ere you go to bed;   15

III.4.2. **move:** persuade (to marry Paris).
11.   **mewed up to her heaviness:** shut away because of her great grief.
12.   **desperate tender:** bold offer.

Acquaint her here of my son Paris' love
And bid her (mark you me?) on Wednesday next—
But soft! What day is this?

Paris.   Monday, my lord.

Capulet.

Monday! Ha, ha! Well, Wednesday is too soon.
A' Thursday let it be—a' Thursday, tell her,   20
She shall be married to this noble earl.
Will you be ready? Do you like this haste?
We'll keep no great ado—a friend or two;
For hark you, Tybalt being slain so late,
It may be thought we held him carelessly,   25
Being our kinsman, if we revel much.
Therefore we'll have some half a dozen friends,
And there an end. But what say you to Thursday?

Paris.

My lord, I would that Thursday were tomorrow.

Capulet.

Well, get you gone. A' Thursday be it then.   30
Go you to Juliet ere you go to bed;
Prepare her, wife, against this wedding day.
Farewell, my lord.—Light to my chamber, ho!
Afore me,° it is so very late
That we may call it early by and by.   35
Good night.   [*Exeunt.*]

Scene 5. *Capulet's orchard.*

Enter ROMEO *and* JULIET *aloft.*

Juliet.

Wilt thou be gone? It is not yet near day.
It was the nightingale, and not the lark,

---

34. **Afore me:** in truth.

That pierced the fearful hollow of thine ear.
Nightly she sings on yond pomegranate tree.
Believe me, love, it was the nightingale.   5
Romeo.
It was the lark, the herald of the morn;
No nightingale. Look, love, what envious streaks
Do lace the severing clouds in yonder east.
Night's candles are burnt out, and jocund day
Stands tiptoe on the misty mountaintops.   10
I must be gone and live, or stay and die.
Juliet.
Yond light is not daylight; I know it, I.
It is some meteor that the sun exhales°
To be to thee this night a torchbearer
And light thee on thy way to Mantua.   15
Therefore stay yet; thou need'st not to be gone.
Romeo.
Let me be taken, let me be put to death.
I am content, so thou wilt have it so.
I'll say yon gray is not the morning's eye,
'Tis but the pale reflex° of Cynthia's brow;°   20
Nor that is not the lark whose notes do beat
The vaulty heaven so high above our heads.
I have more care to stay than will to go.
Come, death, and welcome! Juliet wills it so.
How is't, my soul? Let's talk; it is not day.   25
Juliet.
It is, it is! Hie hence, be gone, away!
It is the lark that sings so out of tune,
Straining harsh discords and unpleasing sharps.
Some say the lark makes sweet division;°
This doth not so, for she divideth us.   30

III.5.13. **exhales:** gives off. (It was believed that the sun drew up vapors
and ignited them as meteors.)
20.   **reflex:** reflection. **Cynthia's brow:** Cynthia is the moon.
29.   **division:** literally, a rapid run of notes, but Juliet is punning on the
word's other meaning (separation).

Some say the lark and loathèd toad change eyes;°
O, now I would they had changed voices too,
Since arm from arm that voice doth us affray,°
Hunting thee hence with hunt's-up° to the day.
O, now be gone! More light and light it grows.   35
Romeo.
More light and light—more dark and dark our woes.

Enter NURSE.

Nurse. Madam!
Juliet. Nurse?
Nurse.
Your lady mother is coming to your chamber.
The day is broke; be wary, look about.   [*Exit.*]   40
Juliet.
Then, window, let day in, and let life out.
Romeo.
Farewell, farewell! One kiss, and I'll descend.

He goes down.

Juliet.
Art thou gone so, love-lord, ay husband-friend?
I must hear from thee every day in the hour,
For in a minute there are many days.   45
O, for this count I shall be much in years
Ere I again behold my Romeo!
Romeo.
Farewell!
I will omit no opportunity
That may convey my greetings, love, to thee.   50
Juliet.
O, think'st thou we shall ever meet again?

---

31. A fable tells why the lark, which sings so beautifully, has ugly eyes,
    and why the toad, which croaks so harshly, has beautiful ones.
33. **affray:** frighten.
34. **hunt's-up:** hunter's morning song.

Romeo.
I doubt it not; and all these woes shall serve
For sweet discourses in our times to come.
Juliet.
O God, I have an ill-divining soul!
Methinks I see thee, now thou art so low,   55
As one dead in the bottom of a tomb.
Either my eyesight fails, or thou look'st pale.
Romeo.
And trust me, love, in my eye so do you.
Dry° sorrow drinks our blood. Adieu, adieu! [*Exit.*]
Juliet.
O Fortune, Fortune! All men call thee fickle.   60
If thou art fickle, what dost thou with him
That is renowned for faith? Be fickle, Fortune,
For then I hope thou wilt not keep him long
But send him back.

Enter Juliet's mother, LADY CAPULET.

Lady Capulet.
Ho, daughter! Are you up?   65
Juliet.
Who is't that calls? It is my lady mother.
Is she not down so late,° or up so early?
What unaccustomed cause procures her hither?
Lady Capulet.
Why, how now, Juliet?
Juliet.   Madam, I am not well.
Lady Capulet.
Evermore weeping for your cousin's death?   70
What, wilt thou wash him from his grave with tears?
And if thou couldst, thou couldst not make him live.
Therefore have done. Some grief shows much of love;
But much of grief shows still some want of wit.

---

59. **Dry:** thirsty (sorrow was thought to drain color from the cheeks).
67. **down so late:** so late getting to bed.

Juliet.
Yet let me weep for such a feeling loss.°   75
Lady Capulet.
So shall you feel the loss, but not the friend
Which you weep for.
Juliet.   Feeling so the loss,
I cannot choose but ever weep the friend.
Lady Capulet.
Well, girl, thou weep'st not so much for his death
As that the villain lives which slaughtered him.   80
Juliet.
What villain, madam?
Lady Capulet.   That same villain Romeo.
Juliet [*aside*].
Villain and he be many miles asunder—
God pardon him! I do, with all my heart;
And yet no man like he doth grieve my heart.
Lady Capulet.
That is because the traitor murderer lives.   85
Juliet.
Ay, madam, from the reach of these my hands.
Would none but I might venge my cousin's death!
Lady Capulet.
We will have vengeance for it, fear thou not.
Then weep no more. I'll send to one in Mantua,
Where that same banished runagate° doth live,   90
Shall give him such an unaccustomed dram°
That he shall soon keep Tybalt company;
And then I hope thou wilt be satisfied.
Juliet.
Indeed I never shall be satisfied
With Romeo till I behold him—dead—   95
Is my poor heart so for a kinsman vexed.

---

75. feeling loss: loss so deeply felt.
90. runagate: fugitive.
91. unaccustomed dram: unexpected drink (of poison).

Madam, if you could find out but a man
To bear a poison, I would temper° it—
That Romeo should, upon receipt thereof,
Soon sleep in quiet. O, how my heart abhors   100
To hear him named and cannot come to him,
To wreak° the love I bore my cousin
Upon his body that hath slaughtered him!
Lady Capulet.
Find thou the means, and I'll find such a man.
But now I'll tell thee joyful tidings, girl.   105
Juliet.
And joy comes well in such a needy time.
What are they, I beseech your ladyship?
Lady Capulet.
Well, well, thou hast a careful° father, child;
One who, to put thee from thy heaviness,
Hath sorted out° a sudden day of joy   110
That thou expects not nor I looked not for.
Juliet.
Madam, in happy time!° What day is that?
Lady Capulet.
Marry, my child, early next Thursday morn
The gallant, young, and noble gentleman,
The County Paris, at Saint Peter's Church,   115
Shall happily make thee there a joyful bride.
Juliet.
Now by Saint Peter's Church, and Peter too,
He shall not make me there a joyful bride!
I wonder at this haste, that I must wed
Ere he that should be husband comes to woo.   120
I pray you tell my lord and father, madam,
I will not marry yet; and when I do, I swear

---

98. **temper:** mix (she really means "weaken").
102. **wreak:** avenge (she really means "express").
108. **careful:** full of caring (for Juliet).
110. **sorted out:** chosen.
112. **in happy time:** at a lucky time.

It shall be Romeo, whom you know I hate,
Rather than Paris. These are news indeed!
Lady Capulet.
    Here comes your father. Tell him so yourself,   125
    And see how he will take it at your hands.

Enter CAPULET *and* NURSE.

Capulet.
    When the sun sets the earth doth drizzle dew,
    But for the sunset of my brother's son
    It rains downright.
    How now? A conduit,° girl? What, still in tears?   130
    Evermore showering? In one little body
    Thou counterfeits a bark,° a sea, a wind:
    For still thy eyes, which I may call the sea,
    Do ebb and flow with tears; the bark thy body is,
    Sailing in this salt flood; the winds, thy sighs,   135
    Who, raging with thy tears and they with them,
    Without a sudden calm will overset
    Thy tempest-tossèd body. How now, wife?
    Have you delivered to her our decree?
Lady Capulet.
    Ay, sir; but she will none, she gives you thanks.   140
    I would the fool were married to her grave!
Capulet.
    Soft! Take me with you,° take me with you, wife.
    How? Will she none? Doth she not give us thanks?
    Is she not proud? Doth she not count her blest,
    Unworthy as she is, that we have wrought°   145
    So worthy a gentleman to be her bride?

---

130. **conduit:** fountain (Juliet is weeping).
132. **counterfeits a bark:** imitates a boat.
142. **Soft! Take me with you:** Wait! What do you mean?
145. **wrought:** arranged.

Juliet.

Not proud you have, but thankful that you have.

Proud can I never be of what I hate,

But thankful even for hate that is meant love.

Capulet.

How, how, how, how, chopped-logic?° What is this? 150

"Proud"—and "I thank you"—and "I thank you not"—

And yet "not proud"? Mistress minion° you,

Thank me no thankings, nor proud me no prouds,

But fettle° your fine joints 'gainst Thursday next

To go with Paris to Saint Peter's Church, 155

Or I will drag thee on a hurdle thither.

Out, you greensickness carrion! Out, you baggage!

You tallow-face!

Lady Capulet.   Fie, fie! What, are you mad?

Juliet.

Good father, I beseech you on my knees,

Hear me with patience but to speak a word. 160

Capulet.

Hang thee, young baggage! Disobedient wretch!

I tell thee what—get thee to church a' Thursday

Or never after look me in the face.

Speak not, reply not, do not answer me!

My fingers itch. Wife, we scarce thought us blest 165

That God had lent us but this only child;

But now I see this one is one too much,

And that we have a curse in having her.

Out on her, hilding!

Nurse.   God in heaven bless her!

You are to blame, my lord, to rate° her so. 170

---

150. **chopped-logic:** hairsplitting.
152. **minion:** badly behaved girl.
154. **fettle:** prepare.
170. **rate:** berate, scold.

Capulet.
  And why, my Lady Wisdom? Hold your tongue,
  Good Prudence. Smatter with your gossips,° go!
Nurse.
  I speak no treason.
Capulet.   O, God-i-god-en!°
Nurse.
  May not one speak?
Capulet.   Peace, you mumbling fool!
  Utter your gravity o'er a gossip's bowl,   175
  For here we need it not.
Lady Capulet.   You are too hot.
Capulet.
  God's bread!° It makes me mad.
  Day, night; hour, tide, time; work, play;
  Alone, in company; still my care hath been
  To have her matched; and having now provided   180
  A gentleman of noble parentage,
  Of fair demesnes, youthful, and nobly trained,
  Stuffed, as they say, with honorable parts,
  Proportioned as one's thought would wish a man—
  And then to have a wretched puling° fool,   185
  A whining mammet,° in her fortune's tender,°
  To answer "I'll not wed, I cannot love;
  I am too young, I pray you pardon me"!
  But, and you will not wed, I'll pardon you!°
  Graze where you will, you shall not house with me.   190
  Look to't, think on't; I do not use to jest.
  Thursday is near; lay hand on heart, advise.°

---

172. **Smatter with your gossips:** chatter with your gossipy friends.
173. **God-i-god-en!:** Get on with you! ("God give you good evening.")
177. **God's bread!:** oath on the sacrament of Communion.
185. **puling:** whimpering.
186. **mammet:** doll. **in her fortune's tender:** when good fortune is offered to her.
189. **I'll pardon you!:** I'll give you permission to go!
192. **advise:** consider.

And you be mine, I'll give you to my friend;
And you be not, hang, beg, starve, die in the streets,
For, by my soul, I'll ne'er acknowledge thee,   195
Nor what is mine shall never do thee good.
Trust to't. Bethink you. I'll not be forsworn.°   [*Exit.*]
Juliet.
Is there no pity sitting in the clouds
That sees into the bottom of my grief?
O sweet my mother, cast me not away!   200
Delay this marriage for a month, a week;
Or if you do not, make the bridal bed
In that dim monument where Tybalt lies.
Lady Capulet.
Talk not to me, for I'll not speak a word.
Do as thou wilt, for I have done with thee.   [*Exit.*]   205
Juliet.
O God!—O nurse, how shall this be prevented?
My husband is on earth, my faith in heaven.°
How shall that faith return again to earth
Unless that husband send it me from heaven
By leaving earth? Comfort me, counsel me.   210
Alack, alack, that heaven should practice stratagems
Upon so soft a subject as myself!
What say'st thou? Hast thou not a word of joy?
Some comfort, nurse.
Nurse.   Faith, here it is.
Romeo is banished; and all the world to nothing°   215
That he dares ne'er come back to challenge you;
Or if he do, it needs must be by stealth.
Then, since the case so stands as now it doth,
I think it best you married with the county.
O, he's a lovely gentleman!   220

---

197. forsworn: guilty of breaking his vow.
207. my faith in heaven: my wedding vow is recorded in heaven.
215. all the world to nothing: it is a safe bet.

Romeo's a dishclout° to him. An eagle, madam,
Hath not so green, so quick, so fair an eye
As Paris hath. Beshrew° my very heart,
I think you are happy in this second match,
For it excels your first; or if it did not,   225
Your first is dead—or 'twere as good he were
As living here and you no use of him.
Juliet.
Speak'st thou from thy heart?
Nurse.
And from my soul too; else beshrew them both.
Juliet. Amen!   230
Nurse. What?
Juliet.
Well, thou hast comforted me marvelous much.
Go in; and tell my lady I am gone,
Having displeased my father, to Laurence' cell,
To make confession and to be absolved.   235
Nurse.
Marry, I will; and this is wisely done.   [*Exit.*]
Juliet.
Ancient damnation!° O most wicked fiend!
Is it more sin to wish me thus forsworn,
Or to dispraise my lord with that same tongue
Which she hath praised him with above compare   240
So many thousand times? Go, counselor!
Thou and my bosom henceforth shall be twain.°
I'll to the friar to know his remedy.
If all else fail, myself have power to die.   [*Exit.*]

---

221. **dishclout:** literally dishcloth; limp and weak.
223. **Beshrew:** curse.
237. **Ancient damnation!:** Old devil!
242. **twain:** separate.

Act IV

Scene 1. *Friar Laurence's cell.*

Enter FRIAR LAURENCE *and* COUNT PARIS.

Friar.
On Thursday, sir? The time is very short.
Paris.
My father Capulet will have it so,
And I am nothing slow to slack his haste.
Friar.
You say you do not know the lady's mind.
Uneven° is the course; I like it not.   5
Paris.
Immoderately she weeps for Tybalt's death,
And therefore have I little talked of love;
For Venus smiles not in a house of tears.
Now, sir, her father counts it dangerous
That she do give her sorrow so much sway,   10
And in his wisdom hastes our marriage
To stop the inundation of her tears,
Which, too much minded° by herself alone,
May be put from her by society.
Now do you know the reason of this haste.   15
Friar [*aside*].
I would I knew not why it should be slowed,—
Look, sir, here comes the lady toward my cell.

IV.1.5. **Uneven:** irregular or unusual.
13.   **minded:** brooded over.

107

Enter JULIET.

Paris.

Happily met, my lady and my wife!

Juliet.

That may be, sir, when I may be a wife.

Paris.

That "may be" must be, love, on Thursday next.   20

Juliet.

What must be shall be.

Friar.   That's a certain text.

Paris.

Come you to make confession to this father?

Juliet.

To answer that, I should confess to you.

Paris.

Do not deny to him that you love me.

Juliet.

I will confess to you that I love him.   25

Paris.

So will ye, I am sure, that you love me.

Juliet.

If I do so, it will be of more price,

Being spoke behind your back, than to your face.

Paris.

Poor soul, thy face is much abused with tears.

Juliet.

The tears have got small victory by that,   30

For it was bad enough before their spite.°

Paris.

Thou wrong'st it more than tears with that report.

Juliet.

That is no slander, sir, which is a truth;

And what I spake, I spake it to my face.

---

31. **spite:** injury or damage (to her face).

Paris.
　Thy face is mine, and thou hast slandered it.　　　　35
Juliet.
　It may be so, for it is not mine own.
　Are you at leisure, holy father, now,
　Or shall I come to you at evening mass?
Friar.
　My leisure serves me, pensive daughter, now.
　My lord, we must entreat the time alone.　　　　40
Paris.
　God shield° I should disturb devotion!
　Juliet, on Thursday early will I rouse ye.
　Till then, adieu, and keep this holy kiss.　　　[*Exit.*]
Juliet.
　O, shut the door, and when thou hast done so,
　Come weep with me—past hope, past care, past help!　45
Friar.
　O Juliet, I already know thy grief;
　It strains me past the compass of my wits.
　I hear thou must, and nothing may prorogue° it,
　On Thursday next be married to this county.
Juliet.
　Tell me not, friar, that thou hearest of this,　　　50
　Unless thou tell me how I may prevent it.
　If in thy wisdom thou canst give no help,
　Do thou but call my resolution wise
　And with this knife I'll help it presently.
　God joined my heart and Romeo's, thou our hands;　55
　And ere this hand, by thee to Romeo's sealed,
　Shall be the label° to another deed,°
　Or my true heart with treacherous revolt
　Turn to another, this shall slay them both.

---

41. **God shield:** God forbid.
48. **prorogue:** postpone.
57. **label:** seal. **deed:** contract (of marriage).

Therefore, out of thy long-experienced time,　　　　60
Give me some present counsel; or, behold,
'Twixt my extremes and me this bloody knife
Shall play the umpire, arbitrating that
Which the commission° of thy years and art
Could to no issue of true honor bring.　　　　　　65
Be not so long to speak. I long to die
If what thou speak'st speak not of remedy.
Friar.
Hold, daughter. I do spy a kind of hope,
Which craves as desperate an execution
As that is desperate which we would prevent.　　70
If, rather than to marry County Paris,
Thou hast the strength of will to slay thyself,
Then is it likely thou wilt undertake
A thing like death to chide away this shame,
That cop'st° with death himself to scape from it;　75
And, if thou darest, I'll give thee remedy.
Juliet.
O, bid me leap, rather than marry Paris,
From off the battlements of any tower,
Or walk in thievish ways, or bid me lurk
Where serpents are; chain me with roaring bears,　80
Or hide me nightly in a charnel house,°
O'ercovered quite with dead men's rattling bones,
With reeky° shanks and yellow chapless° skulls;
Or bid me go into a new-made grave
And hide me with a dead man in his shroud—　　85
Things that, to hear them told, have made me
　　tremble—
And I will do it without fear or doubt,
To live an unstained wife to my sweet love.

---

64. commission: authority.
75. cop'st: negotiates.
81. charnel house: house where bones from old graves are kept.
83. reeky: stinking. **chapless:** jawless.

Friar.

Hold, then. Go home, be merry, give consent
To marry Paris. Wednesday is tomorrow.   90
Tomorrow night look that thou lie alone;
Let not the nurse lie with thee in thy chamber.
Take thou this vial, being then in bed,
And this distilling° liquor drink thou off;
When presently through all thy veins shall run   95
A cold and drowsy humor;° for no pulse
Shall keep his native° progress, but surcease;°
No warmth, no breath, shall testify thou livest;
The roses in thy lips and cheeks shall fade
To wanny° ashes, thy eyes' windows fall   100
Like death when he shuts up the day of life;
Each part, deprived of supple government,°
Shall, stiff and stark and cold, appear like death;
And in this borrowed likeness of shrunk death
Thou shalt continue two-and-forty hours,   105
And then awake as from a pleasant sleep.
Now, when the bridegroom in the morning comes
To rouse thee from thy bed, there art thou dead.
Then, as the manner of our country is,
In thy best robes uncovered on the bier   110
Thou shalt be borne to that same ancient vault
Where all the kindred of the Capulets lie.
In the meantime, against° thou shalt awake,
Shall Romeo by my letters know our drift;°
And hither shall he come; and he and I   115
Will watch thy waking, and that very night
Shall Romeo bear thee hence to Mantua.

---

94. **distilling:** penetrating.
96. **humor:** liquid.
97. **native:** natural. **surcease:** cease.
100. **wanny:** pale.
102. **government:** control.
113. **against:** before.
114. **drift:** intentions.

And this shall free thee from this present shame,
If no inconstant toy° nor womanish fear
Abate thy valor in the acting it.   120
Juliet.
Give me, give me! O, tell not me of fear!
Friar.
Hold! Get you gone, be strong and prosperous
In this resolve. I'll send a friar with speed
To Mantua, with my letters to thy lord.
Juliet.
Love give me strength, and strength shall help afford.   125
Farewell, dear father.   [*Exit with* FRIAR.]

Scene 2. *A hall in Capulet's house.*

Enter father CAPULET, LADY CAPULET, NURSE, *and*
SERVINGMEN, *two or three.*

Capulet.
So many guests invite as here are writ.

Exit a SERVINGMAN.

Sirrah, go hire me twenty cunning° cooks.
Servingman. You shall have none ill, sir; for I'll try if
they can lick their fingers.
Capulet.
How canst thou try them so?   5
Servingman. Marry, sir, 'tis an ill cook that cannot lick
his own fingers. Therefore he that cannot lick his
fingers goes not with me.

---

119. **toy:** whim.
IV.2.2. **cunning:** skillful.

Capulet. Go, be gone.   [*Exit* SERVINGMAN.]
We shall be much unfurnished° for this time.   10
What, is my daughter gone to Friar Laurence?
Nurse. Ay, forsooth.
Capulet.
Well, he may chance to do some good on her.
A peevish self-willed harlotry it is.

Enter JULIET.

Nurse.
See where she comes from shrift with merry look.   15
Capulet.
How now, my headstrong? Where have you been
    gadding?
Juliet.
Where I have learnt me to repent the sin
Of disobedient opposition
To you and your behests, and am enjoined
By holy Laurence to fall prostrate here   20
To beg your pardon. Pardon, I beseech you!
Henceforward I am ever ruled by you.
Capulet.
Send for the county. Go tell him of this.
I'll have this knot knit up tomorrow morning.
Juliet.
I met the youthful lord at Laurence' cell   25
And gave him what becomèd° love I might,
Not stepping o'er the bounds of modesty.
Capulet.
Why, I am glad on't. This is well. Stand up.
This is as't should be. Let me see the county.
Ay, marry, go, I say, and fetch him hither.   30

---

10. **unfurnished:** unsupplied (without food).
26. **becomèd:** suitable.

Now, afore God, this reverend holy friar,
All our whole city is much bound to him.
Juliet.
Nurse, will you go with me into my closet,°
To help me sort such needful ornaments
As you think fit to furnish me tomorrow?   35
Lady Capulet.
No, not till Thursday. There is time enough.
Capulet.
Go, nurse, go with her. We'll to church tomorrow.

Exeunt JULIET *and* NURSE.

Lady Capulet.
We shall be short in our provision.
'Tis now near night.
Capulet.   Tush, I will stir about,
And all things shall be well, I warrant thee, wife.   40
Go thou to Juliet, help to deck up her.
I'll not to bed tonight; let me alone.
I'll play the housewife for this once. What, ho!
They are all forth; well, I will walk myself
To County Paris, to prepare up him   45
Against tomorrow. My heart is wondrous light,
Since this same wayward girl is so reclaimed.

Exit with LADY CAPULET.

Scene 3. *Juliet's chamber.*

Enter JULIET *and* NURSE.

Juliet.
Ay, those attires are best; but, gentle nurse,
I pray thee leave me to myself tonight;

---

33. **closet:** private room.

For I have need of many orisons°
To move the heavens to smile upon my state,
Which, well thou knowest, is cross and full of sin.   5

Enter LADY CAPULET.

Lady Capulet.
    What, are you busy, ho? Need you my help?
Juliet.
    No, madam; we have culled such necessaries
    As are behoveful° for our state° tomorrow.
    So please you, let me now be left alone,
    And let the nurse this night sit up with you;   10
    For I am sure you have your hands full all
    In this so sudden business.
Lady Capulet.   Good night.
    Get thee to bed, and rest; for thou hast need.

                    Exeunt LADY CAPULET *and* NURSE.

Juliet.
    Farewell! God knows when we shall meet again.
    I have a faint cold fear thrills through my veins   15
    That almost freezes up the heat of life.
    I'll call them back again to comfort me.
    Nurse!—What should she do here?
    My dismal scene I needs must act alone.
    Come, vial.   20
    What if this mixture do not work at all?
    Shall I be married then tomorrow morning?
    No, no! This shall forbid it. Lie thou there.

Lays down a dagger.

    What if it be a poison which the friar
    Subtly hath ministered to have me dead,   25
    Lest in this marriage he should be dishonored

IV.3.3.   **orisons:** prayers.
8.   **behoveful:** suitable. **state:** ceremonies.

Because he married me before to Romeo?
I fear it is; and yet methinks it should not,
For he hath still been tried° a holy man.
How if, when I am laid into the tomb,   30
I wake before the time that Romeo
Come to redeem me? There's a fearful point!
Shall I not then be stifled in the vault,
To whose foul mouth no healthsome air breathes in,
And there die strangled ere my Romeo comes?   35
Or, if I live, is it not very like
The horrible conceit of death and night,
Together with the terror of the place—
As in a vault, an ancient receptacle
Where for this many hundred years the bones   40
Of all my buried ancestors are packed;
Where bloody Tybalt, yet but green in earth,°
Lies fest'ring in his shroud; where, as they say,
At some hours in the night spirits resort—
Alack, alack, is it not like that I,   45
So early waking—what with loathsome smells,
And shrieks like mandrakes° torn out of the earth,
That living mortals, hearing them, run mad—
I, if I wake, shall I not be distraught,
Environèd with all these hideous fears,   50
And madly play with my forefathers' joints,
And pluck the mangled Tybalt from his shroud,
And, in this rage, with some great kinsman's bone
As with a club dash out my desp'rate brains?
O, look! Methinks I see my cousin's ghost   55
Seeking out Romeo, that did spit his body
Upon a rapier's point. Stay, Tybalt, stay!
Romeo, Romeo, Romeo, I drink to thee.

She falls upon her bed within the curtains.

---

29. **still been tried:** always been proved.
42. **green in earth:** newly buried.
47. **mandrakes:** plants resembling the human body, which were said to
     grow beneath the gallows and to scream when torn up.

Scene 4. *A hall in Capulet's house.*

Enter LADY CAPULET *and* NURSE.

Lady Capulet.
Hold, take these keys and fetch more spices, nurse.
Nurse.
They call for dates and quinces in the pastry.

Enter old CAPULET.

Capulet.
Come, stir, stir, stir! The second cock hath crowed,
The curfew bell hath rung, 'tis three o'clock.
Look to the baked meats, good Angelica;   5
Spare not for cost.
Nurse.   Go, you cotquean,° go,
Get you to bed! Faith, you'll be sick tomorrow
For this night's watching.
Capulet.
No, not a whit. What, I have watched ere now
All night for lesser cause, and ne'er been sick.   10
Lady Capulet.
Ay, you have been a mouse hunt° in your time;
But I will watch you from such watching now.

                    Exeunt LADY CAPULET *and* NURSE.

Capulet.
A jealous hood,° a jealous hood!

Enter three or four FELLOWS *with spits and logs and baskets.*

                            Now, fellow,
What is there?
First Fellow.
Things for the cook, sir; but I know not what.   15

IV.4.6. cotquean: old woman (a man who acts like an old woman).
11.   mouse hunt: woman-chaser or night prowler.
13.   hood: female.

Capulet.

Make haste, make haste.   [*Exit* FIRST FELLOW.]

Sirrah, fetch drier logs.

Call Peter; he will show thee where they are.

Second Fellow.

I have a head, sir, that will find out logs°

And never trouble Peter for the matter.

Capulet.

Mass,° and well said; a merry whoreson, ha!   20

Thou shalt be loggerhead.°

Exit SECOND FELLOW, *with the others.*

Good faith, 'tis day.

The county will be here with music straight,

For so he said he would. [*Play music offstage.*]

I hear him near.

Nurse! Wife! What, ho! What, nurse, I say!

Enter NURSE.

Go waken Juliet; go and trim her up.   25

I'll go and chat with Paris. Hie, make haste,

Make haste! The bridegroom he is come already:

Make haste, I say.   [*Exit.*]

Scene 5. *Juliet's chamber.*

Nurse.

Mistress! What, mistress! Juliet! Fast,° I warrant her, she.

Why, lamb! Why, lady! Fie, you slugabed.

Why, love, I say! Madam; sweetheart! Why, bride!

What, not a word? You take your pennyworths° now;

---

18.   I . . . logs: in other words, "I have a wooden head."
20.   **Mass:** mild oath, short for "by the Mass."
21.   **loggerhead:** stupid person.
IV.5.1.   **Fast:** fast asleep.
 4.   **pennyworths:** small naps.

Sleep for a week; for the next night, I warrant,   5
The County Paris hath set up his rest°
That you shall rest but little. God forgive me!
Marry, and amen. How sound is she asleep!
I needs must wake her. Madam, madam, madam!
Ay, let the county take you in your bed;   10
He'll fright you up, i' faith. Will it not be?

Draws aside the curtains.

What, dressed, and in your clothes, and down again?
I must needs wake you. Lady! Lady! Lady!
Alas, alas! Help, help! My lady's dead!
O weraday that ever I was born!   15
Some aqua vitae, ho! My lord! My lady!

Enter LADY CAPULET.

Lady Capulet.
What noise is here?
Nurse.   O lamentable day!
Lady Capulet.
What is the matter?
Nurse.   Look, look! O heavy day!
Lady Capulet.
O me, O me! My child, my only life!
Revive, look up, or I will die with thee!   20
Help, help! Call help.

Enter CAPULET.

Capulet.
For shame, bring Juliet forth; her lord is come.
Nurse.
She's dead, deceased; she's dead, alack the day!
Lady Capulet.
Alack the day, she's dead, she's dead, she's dead!

---

6. **set up his rest:** become firmly resolved.

Capulet.
Ha! Let me see her. Out, alas! She's cold,   25
Her blood is settled, and her joints are stiff;
Life and these lips have long been separated.
Death lies on her like an untimely frost
Upon the sweetest flower of all the field.
Nurse.
O lamentable day!
Lady Capulet.   O woeful time!   30
Capulet.
Death, that hath ta'en her hence to make me wail,
Ties up my tongue and will not let me speak.

Enter FRIAR LAURENCE *and* PARIS, *with* MUSICIANS.

Friar.
Come, is the bride ready to go to church?
Capulet.
Ready to go, but never to return.
O son, the night before thy wedding day   35
Hath Death lain with thy wife. There she lies,
Flower as she was, deflowerèd by him.
Death is my son-in-law, Death is my heir;
My daughter he hath wedded. I will die
And leave him all. Life, living, all is Death's.   40
Paris.
Have I thought, love, to see this morning's face,
And doth it give me such a sight as this?
Lady Capulet.
Accursed, unhappy, wretched, hateful day!
Most miserable hour that e'er time saw
In lasting labor of his pilgrimage!   45
But one, poor one, one poor and loving child,
But one thing to rejoice and solace in,
And cruel Death hath catched it from my sight.
Nurse.
O woe! O woeful, woeful, woeful day!
Most lamentable day, most woeful day   50

That ever ever I did yet behold!
O day, O day, O day! O hateful day!
Never was seen so black a day as this.
O woeful day! O woeful day!

Paris.

Beguiled, divorcèd, wrongèd, spited, slain!   55
Most detestable Death, by thee beguiled,
By cruel, cruel thee quite overthrown.
O love! O life!—not life, but love in death!

Capulet.

Despised, distressèd, hated, martyred, killed!
Uncomfortable time, why cam'st thou now   60
To murder, murder our solemnity?
O child, O child! My soul, and not my child!
Dead art thou—alack, my child is dead,
And with my child my joys are burièd!

Friar.

Peace, ho, for shame! Confusion's cure lives not   65
In these confusions. Heaven and yourself
Had part in this fair maid—now heaven hath all,
And all the better is it for the maid.
Your part in her you could not keep from death,
But heaven keeps his part in eternal life.   70
The most you sought was her promotion,
For 'twas your heaven she should be advanced;
And weep ye now, seeing she is advanced
Above the clouds, as high as heaven itself?
O, in this love, you love your child so ill   75
That you run mad, seeing that she is well.°
She's not well married that lives married long,
But she's best married that dies married young.
Dry up your tears and stick your rosemary°
On this fair corse, and, as the custom is,   80
And in her best array bear her to church;

---

76. **well:** that is, she is in heaven.
79. **rosemary:** herb that stands for remembrance.

For though fond nature° bids us all lament,
Yet nature's tears are reason's merriment.
Capulet.
 All things that we ordainèd festival
 Turn from their office to black funeral—   85
 Our instruments to melancholy bells,
 Our wedding cheer to a sad burial feast;
 Our solemn hymns to sullen dirges change;
 Our bridal flowers serve for a buried corse;
 And all things change them to the contrary.   90
Friar.
 Sir, go you in; and, madam, go with him;
 And go, Sir Paris. Everyone prepare
 To follow this fair corse unto her grave.
 The heavens do lower° upon you for some ill;
 Move them no more by crossing their high will.   95

Exeunt, casting rosemary on her and shutting the curtains.
The NURSE *and* MUSICIANS *remain.*

First Musician.
 Faith, we may put up our pipes and be gone.
Nurse.
 Honest good fellows, ah, put up, put up!
 For well you know this is a pitiful case.   [*Exit.*]
First Musician.
 Ay, by my troth, the case may be amended.

Enter PETER.

Peter. Musicians, O, musicians, "Heart's ease," "Heart's 100
 ease"! O, and you will have me live, play "Heart's
 ease."
First Musician. Why "Heart's ease"?

---

82. **fond nature:** silly human nature.
94. **lower:** frown.

Peter. O, musicians, because my heart itself plays "My
heart is full." O, play me some merry dump° to com-   105
fort me.

First Musician. Not a dump we! 'Tis no time to play
now.

Peter. You will not then?

First Musician. No.   110

Peter. I will then give it you soundly.

First Musician. What will you give us?

Peter. No money, on my faith, but the gleek.° I will give
you° the minstrel.

First Musician. Then will I give you the serving-   115
creature.

Peter. Then will I lay the serving-creature's dagger on
your pate. I will carry° no crotchets. I'll re you, I'll fa
you. Do you note me?

First Musician. And you re us and fa us, you note us.   120

Second Musician. Pray you put up your dagger, and
put out your wit. Then have at you with my wit!

Peter. I will dry-beat° you with an iron wit, and put up
my iron dagger. Answer me like men.

"When griping grief the heart doth wound,   125
And doleful dumps the mind oppress,
Then music with her silver sound"—

Why "silver sound"? Why "music with her silver
sound"? What say you, Simon Catling?°

First Musician. Marry, sir, because silver hath a sweet   130
sound.

Peter. Pretty! What say you, Hugh Rebeck?°

---

105. **dump:** sad song.
113. **gleek:** jeer or insult.
113–114. **give you:** call you (to be called a minstrel was an insult to a
musician).
118. **carry:** put up with.
123. **dry-beat:** beat soundly.
129. **Catling:** lute string.
132. **Rebeck:** fiddle.

Second Musician. I say "silver sound" because musicians
  sound for silver.
Peter. Pretty too! What say you, James Soundpost?°   135
Third Musician. Faith, I know not what to say.
Peter. O, I cry you mercy,° you are the singer. I will say
  for you. It is "music with her silver sound" because
  musicians have no gold for sounding.°
  "Then music with her silver sound   140
  With speedy help doth lend redress."   [*Exit.*]
First Musician. What a pestilent knave is this same!
Second Musician. Hang him, Jack! Come, we'll in here,
  tarry for the mourners, and stay dinner.

                    Exit with others.

---

135. **Soundpost:** post inside a violin or similar instrument that provides
    support.
137. **cry you mercy:** beg your pardon.
139. **no gold for sounding:** no money to jingle in their pockets.

Act V

Scene 1. *Mantua. A street.*

Enter ROMEO.

Romeo.
    If I may trust the flattering truth of sleep,
    My dreams presage° some joyful news at hand.
    My bosom's lord° sits lightly in his throne,
    And all this day an unaccustomed spirit
    Lifts me above the ground with cheerful thoughts.   5
    I dreamt my lady came and found me dead
    (Strange dream that gives a dead man leave to think!)
    And breathed such life with kisses in my lips
    That I revived and was an emperor.
    Ah me! How sweet is love itself possessed,   10
    When but love's shadows° are so rich in joy!

Enter Romeo's man BALTHASAR, *booted from riding.*

    News from Verona! How now, Balthasar?
    Dost thou not bring me letters from the friar?
    How doth my lady? Is my father well?
    How fares my Juliet? That I ask again,   15
    For nothing can be ill if she be well.
Balthasar.
    Then she is well, and nothing can be ill.
    Her body sleeps in Capel's monument,
    And her immortal part with angels lives.

V.1.2. **presage:** foretell.
  3.   **bosom's lord:** heart.
  11.   **shadows:** dreams.

I saw her laid low in her kindred's vault   20
And presently took post° to tell it you.
O, pardon me for bringing these ill news,
Since you did leave it for my office,° sir.
Romeo.
Is it e'en so? Then I defy you, stars!
Thou knowest my lodging. Get me ink and paper   25
And hire post horses. I will hence tonight.
Balthasar.
I do beseech you, sir, have patience.
Your looks are pale and wild and do import
Some misadventure.
Romeo.   Tush, thou art deceived.
Leave me and do the thing I bid thee do.   30
Hast thou no letters to me from the friar?
Balthasar.
No, my good lord.
Romeo.   No matter. Get thee gone.
And hire those horses. I'll be with thee straight.

                                        Exit BALTHASAR.

Well, Juliet, I will lie with thee tonight.
Let's see for means. O mischief, thou art swift   35
To enter in the thoughts of desperate men!
I do remember an apothecary,
And hereabouts 'a dwells, which late I noted
In tattered weeds,° with overwhelming° brows,
Culling of simples.° Meager were his looks,   40
Sharp misery had worn him to the bones;
And in his needy shop a tortoise hung,
An alligator stuffed, and other skins
Of ill-shaped fishes; and about his shelves

---

21. **post:** horse kept at an inn and rented by travelers.
23. **office:** duty.
39. **weeds:** clothes. **overwhelming:** overhanging.
40. **simples:** herbs.

A beggarly account° of empty boxes,   45
Green earthen pots, bladders, and musty seeds,
Remnants of packthread, and old cakes of roses
Were thinly scatterèd, to make up a show.
Noting this penury,° to myself I said,
"And if a man did need a poison now   50
Whose sale is present death in Mantua,
Here lives a caitiff° wretch would sell it him."
O, this same thought did but forerun my need,
And this same needy man must sell it me.
As I remember, this should be the house.   55
Being holiday, the beggar's shop is shut.
What, ho! Apothecary!

Enter APOTHECARY.

Apothecary.   Who calls so loud?
Romeo.
Come hither, man. I see that thou art poor.
Hold, there is forty ducats. Let me have
A dram of poison, such soon-speeding gear°   60
As will disperse itself through all the veins
That the life-weary taker may fall dead,
And that the trunk° may be discharged of breath
As violently as hasty powder fired
Doth hurry from the fatal cannon's womb.   65
Apothecary.
Such mortal drugs I have; but Mantua's law
Is death to any he that utters° them.
Romeo.
Art thou so bare and full of wretchedness
And fear'st to die? Famine is in thy cheeks,

---

45. account: number.
49. penury: poverty.
52. caitiff: unhappy.
60. gear: stuff.
63. trunk: body.
67. utters: sells.

Need and oppression starveth in thy eyes, 70
Contempt and beggary hangs upon thy back:
The world is not thy friend, nor the world's law;
The world affords no law to make thee rich;
Then be not poor, but break it and take this.

Apothecary.
My poverty but not my will consents. 75

Romeo.
I pay thy poverty and not thy will.

Apothecary.
Put this in any liquid thing you will
And drink it off, and if you had the strength
Of twenty men, it would dispatch you straight.

Romeo.
There is thy gold—worse poison to men's souls, 80
Doing more murder in this loathsome world,
Than these poor compounds that thou mayst not sell.
I sell thee poison; thou has sold me none.
Farewell. Buy food and get thyself in flesh.
Come, cordial and not poison, go with me 85
To Juliet's grave; for there must I use thee. [*Exeunt.*]

Scene 2. *Friar Laurence's cell.*

Enter FRIAR JOHN.

John.
Holy Franciscan friar, brother, ho!

Enter FRIAR LAURENCE.

Laurence.
This same should be the voice of Friar John.
Welcome from Mantua. What says Romeo?
Or, if his mind be writ, give me his letter.

John.
    Going to find a barefoot brother out,   5
    One of our order, to associate° me
    Here in this city visiting the sick,
    And finding him, the searchers° of the town,
    Suspecting that we both were in a house
    Where the infectious pestilence did reign,   10
    Sealed up the doors, and would not let us forth,
    So that my speed to Mantua there was stayed.
Laurence.
    Who bare my letter, then, to Romeo?
John.
    I could not send it—here it is again—
    Nor get a messenger to bring it thee,   15
    So fearful were they of infection.
Laurence.
    Unhappy fortune! By my brotherhood,
    The letter was not nice,° but full of charge,°
    Of dear import; and the neglecting it
    May do much danger. Friar John, go hence,   20
    Get me an iron crow and bring it straight
    Unto my cell.
John.   Brother, I'll go and bring it thee. [*Exit.*]
Laurence.
    Now must I to the monument alone.
    Within this three hours will fair Juliet wake.
    She will beshrew me much that Romeo   25
    Hath had no notice of these accidents;°
    But I will write again to Mantua,
    And keep her at my cell till Romeo come—
    Poor living corse, closed in a dead man's tomb! [*Exit.*]

V.2.6.   **associate:** accompany.
  8.   **searchers:** health officers.
  18.   **nice:** trivial. **charge:** importance.
  26.   **accidents:** events.

Scene 3. *A churchyard; in it, a monument belonging to the Capulets.*

Enter PARIS *and his* PAGE *with flowers and scented water.*

Paris.
    Give me thy torch, boy. Hence, and stand aloof.
    Yet put it out, for I would not be seen.
    Under yond yew trees lay thee all along,°
    Holding the ear close to the hollow ground.
    So shall no foot upon the churchyard tread   5
    (Being loose, unfirm, with digging up of graves)
    But thou shalt hear it. Whistle then to me,
    As signal that thou hear'st something approach.
    Give me those flowers. Do as I bid thee, go.
Page [*aside*].
    I am almost afraid to stand alone   10
    Here in the churchyard; yet I will adventure.°

                          Retires.

Paris.
    Sweet flower, with flowers thy bridal bed I strew
      (O woe! thy canopy is dust and stones)
    Which with sweet water nightly I will dew;
      Or, wanting that, with tears distilled by moans.   15
    The obsequies° that I for thee will keep
    Nightly shall be to strew thy grave and weep.

BOY *whistles.*

    The boy gives warning something doth approach.
    What cursèd foot wanders this way tonight

V.3.3. **all along:** at full length (on the ground).
11. **adventure:** take a chance.
16. **obsequies:** observances or rituals.

To cross° my obsequies and true love's rite?   20
What, with a torch? Muffle° me, night, awhile.

Retires.

Enter ROMEO *and* BALTHASAR *with a torch, a mattock, and a crowbar of iron.*

Romeo.
Give me that mattock and the wrenching iron.
Hold, take this letter. Early in the morning
See thou deliver it to my lord and father.
Give me the light. Upon thy life I charge thee,   25
Whate'er thou hearest or see'st, stand all aloof
And do not interrupt me in my course.
Why I descend into this bed of death
Is partly to behold my lady's face,
But chiefly to take thence from her dead finger   30
A precious ring—a ring that I must use
In dear employment.° Therefore hence, be gone.
But if thou, jealous,° dost return to pry
In what I farther shall intend to do,
By heaven, I will tear thee joint by joint   35
And strew this hungry churchyard with thy limbs.
The time and my intents are savage-wild,
More fierce and more inexorable far
Than empty tigers or the roaring sea.
Balthasar.
I will be gone, sir, and not trouble ye.   40
Romeo.
So shalt thou show me friendship. Take thou that.
Live, and be prosperous; and farewell, good fellow.

---

20. **cross:** thwart.
21. **Muffle:** hide.
32. **In dear employment:** for an important purpose.
33. **jealous:** curious.

Balthasar [*aside*].
    For all this same, I'll hide me hereabout.
    His looks I fear, and his intents I doubt.   [*Retires.*]

Romeo.
    Thou detestable maw,° thou womb of death,   45
    Gorged with the dearest morsel of the earth,
    Thus I enforce thy rotten jaws to open,
    And in despite° I'll cram thee with more food.

ROMEO *opens the tomb.*

Paris.
    This is that banished haughty Montague
    That murd'red my love's cousin—with which grief   50
    It is supposed the fair creature died—
    And here is come to do some villainous shame
    To the dead bodies. I will apprehend him.
    Stop thy unhallowèd toil, vile Montague!
    Can vengeance be pursued further than death?   55
    Condemnèd villain, I do apprehend thee.
    Obey, and go with me; for thou must die.

Romeo.
    I must indeed; and therefore came I hither.
    Good gentle youth, tempt not a desp'rate man.
    Fly hence and leave me. Think upon these gone;   60
    Let them affright thee. I beseech thee, youth,
    Put not another sin upon my head
    By urging me to fury. O, be gone!
    By heaven, I love thee better than myself,
    For I come hither armed against myself.   65
    Stay not, be gone. Live, and hereafter say
    A madman's mercy bid thee run away.

Paris.
    I do defy thy conjurations°
    And apprehend thee for a felon here.

---

45. maw: mouth.
48. in despite: to spite you.
68. conjurations: solemn orders.

Romeo.
Wilt thou provoke me? Then have at thee, boy!   70

They fight.

Page.
O Lord, they fight! I will go call the watch.

Exit. PARIS *falls.*

Paris.
O, I am slain! If thou be merciful,
Open the tomb, lay me with Juliet.   [*Dies.*]
Romeo.
In faith, I will. Let me peruse this face.
Mercutio's kinsman, noble County Paris!   75
What said my man when my betossèd soul
Did not attend° him as we rode? I think
He told me Paris should have married Juliet.
Said he not so, or did I dream it so?
Or am I mad, hearing him talk of Juliet,   80
To think it was so? O, give me thy hand,
One writ with me in sour misfortune's book!
I'll bury thee in a triumphant grave.
A grave? O, no, a lanthorn,° slaught'red youth,
For here lies Juliet, and her beauty makes   85
This vault a feasting presence full of light.
Death, lie thou there, by a dead man interred.

Lays him in the tomb.

How oft when men are at the point of death
Have they been merry! Which their keepers° call
A lightning before death. O, how may I   90
Call this a lightning? O my love, my wife!
Death, that hath sucked the honey of thy breath,
Hath had no power yet upon thy beauty.

---

77. **attend:** listen to.
84. **lanthorn:** a windowed dome.
89. **keepers:** jailers.

Thou art not conquered. Beauty's ensign° yet
Is crimson in thy lips and in thy cheeks,   95
And death's pale flag is not advancèd there.
Tybalt, liest thou there in the bloody sheet?
O, what more favor can I do to thee
Than with that hand that cut thy youth in twain
To sunder his that was thine enemy?   100
Forgive me, cousin! Ah, dear Juliet,
Why art thou yet so fair? Shall I believe
That unsubstantial Death is amorous,
And that the lean abhorrèd monster keeps
Thee here in dark to be his paramour?   105
For fear of that I still will stay with thee
And never from this pallet of dim night
Depart again. Here, here will I remain
With worms that are thy chambermaids. O, here
Will I set up my everlasting rest   110
And shake the yoke of inauspicious stars
From this world-wearied flesh. Eyes, look your last!
Arms, take your last embrace! And, lips, O you
The doors of breath, seal with a righteous kiss
A dateless° bargain to engrossing° death!   115
Come, bitter conduct;° come, unsavory guide!
Thou desperate pilot,° now at once run on
The dashing rocks thy seasick weary bark!
Here's to my love! [*Drinks.*] O true apothecary!
Thy drugs are quick. Thus with a kiss I die.   120

Falls.

Enter FRIAR LAURENCE, *with lanthorn, crowbar, and spade.*

Friar.
　　Saint Francis be my speed! How oft tonight
　　Have my old feet stumbled at graves! Who's there?

---

94. **ensign:** flag (signal).
115. **dateless:** timeless. **engrossing:** all-encompassing.
116. **conduct:** guide (the poison).
117. **desperate pilot:** Romeo himself.

Balthasar.
Here's one, a friend, and one that knows you well.
Friar.
Bliss be upon you! Tell me, good my friend,
What torch is yond that vainly lends his light   125
To grubs and eyeless skulls? As I discern,
It burneth in the Capels' monument.
Balthasar.
It doth so, holy sir; and there's my master,
One that you love.
Friar.   Who is it?
Balthasar.   Romeo.
Friar.
How long hath he been there?
Balthasar.   Full half an hour.   130
Friar.
Go with me to the vault.
Balthasar.   I dare not, sir.
My master knows not but I am gone hence,
And fearfully did menace me with death
If I did stay to look on his intents.
Friar.
Stay then; I'll go alone. Fear comes upon me.   135
O, much I fear some ill unthrifty° thing.
Balthasar.
As I did sleep under this yew tree here,
I dreamt my master and another fought,
And that my master slew him.
Friar.   Romeo!
Alack, alack, what blood is this which stains   140
The stony entrance of this sepulcher?
What mean these masterless and gory swords
To lie discolored by this place of peace?

Enters the tomb.

---

136. **unthrifty:** unlucky.

Romeo! O, pale! Who else? What, Paris too?
And steeped in blood? Ah, what an unkind° hour   145
Is guilty of this lamentable chance!
The lady stirs.

JULIET *rises.*

Juliet.
O comfortable° friar! Where is my lord?
I do remember well where I should be,
And there I am. Where is my Romeo?   150
Friar.
I hear some noise. Lady, come from that nest
Of death, contagion, and unnatural sleep.
A greater power than we can contradict
Hath thwarted our intents. Come, come away.
Thy husband in thy bosom there lies dead;   155
And Paris too. Come, I'll dispose of thee
Among a sisterhood of holy nuns.
Stay not to question, for the watch is coming.
Come, go, good Juliet. I dare no longer stay.
Juliet.
Go, get thee hence, for I will not away.   160

Exit FRIAR.

What's here? A cup, closed in my truelove's hand?
Poison, I see, hath been his timeless° end.
O churl!° Drunk all, and left no friendly drop
To help me after? I will kiss thy lips.
Haply some poison yet doth hang on them   165
To make me die with a restorative.

Kisses him.

Thy lips are warm!

---

145. **unkind:** unnatural.
148. **comfortable:** comforting.
162. **timeless:** untimely.
163. **churl:** rude fellow (spoken teasingly).

Chief Watchman [*within*]. Lead, boy. Which way?
Juliet.
    Yea, noise? Then I'll be brief. O happy° dagger!

Snatches Romeo's dagger.

    This is thy sheath; there rust, and let me die.   170

She stabs herself and falls.

Enter Paris's BOY *and* WATCH.

Boy.
    This is the place. There, where the torch doth burn.
Chief Watchman.
    The ground is bloody. Search about the churchyard.
    Go, some of you; whoe'er you find attach.

                Exeunt some of the WATCH.

    Pitiful sight! Here lies the county slain;
    And Juliet bleeding, warm, and newly dead,   175
    Who here hath lain this two days burièd.
    Go, tell the prince; run to the Capulets;
    Raise up the Montagues; some others search.

                Exeunt others of the WATCH.

    We see the ground whereon these woes do lie,
    But the true ground° of all these piteous woes   180
    We cannot without circumstance° descry.

Enter some of the WATCH, *with Romeo's man* BALTHASAR.

Second Watchman.
    Here's Romeo's man. We found him in the churchyard.
Chief Watchman.
    Hold him in safety till the prince come hither.

---

169. happy: lucky (to be here when she needs it).
180. ground: cause.
181. circumstance: knowledge of the facts.

Enter FRIAR LAURENCE *and another* WATCHMAN.

Third Watchman.
> Here is a friar that trembles, sighs, and weeps.
> We took this mattock and this spade from him   185
> As he was coming from this churchyard's side.

Chief Watchman.
> A great suspicion! Stay the friar too.

Enter the PRINCE *and* ATTENDANTS.

Prince.
> What misadventure is so early up,
> That calls our person from our morning rest?

Enter CAPULET *and his wife,* LADY CAPULET, *with others.*

Capulet.
> What should it be, that is so shrieked abroad?   190

Lady Capulet.
> O, the people in the street cry "Romeo,"
> Some "Juliet," and some "Paris"; and all run
> With open outcry toward our monument.

Prince.
> What fear is this which startles in your ears?

Chief Watchman.
> Sovereign, here lies the County Paris slain;   195
> And Romeo dead; and Juliet, dead before,
> Warm and new killed.

Prince.
> Search, seek, and know how this foul murder comes.

Chief Watchman.
> Here is a friar, and slaughtered Romeo's man,
> With instruments upon them fit to open   200
> These dead men's tombs.

Capulet.
> O heavens! O wife, look how our daughter bleeds!
> This dagger hath mista'en, for, lo, his house°

---

203. house: here, sheath.

Is empty on the back of Montague,
And it missheathèd in my daughter's bosom! 205
Lady Capulet.
O me, this sight of death is as a bell
That warns° my old age to a sepulcher.

Enter MONTAGUE *and others.*

Prince.
Come, Montague; for thou art early up
To see thy son and heir more early down.
Montague.
Alas, my liege, my wife is dead tonight! 210
Grief of my son's exile hath stopped her breath.
What further woe conspires against mine age?
Prince.
Look, and thou shalt see.
Montague.
O thou untaught! What manners is in this,
To press before thy father to a grave? 215
Prince.
Seal up the mouth of outrage for a while,
Till we can clear these ambiguities
And know their spring, their head, their true descent;
And then will I be general of your woes°
And lead you even to death. Meantime forbear, 220
And let mischance be slave to patience.
Bring forth the parties of suspicion.
Friar.
I am the greatest, able to do least,
Yet most suspected, as the time and place
Doth make against me, of this direful murder; 225
And here I stand, both to impeach and purge°
Myself condemnèd and myself excused.

---

207. **warns:** summons.
219. **general of your woes:** leader of your mourning.
226. **impeach and purge:** charge and clear.

Prince.

Then say at once what thou dost know in this.

Friar.

I will be brief, for my short date of breath°
Is not so long as is a tedious tale.   230
Romeo, there dead, was husband to that Juliet;
And she, there dead, that Romeo's faithful wife.
I married them; and their stolen marriage day
Was Tybalt's doomsday, whose untimely death
Banished the new-made bridegroom from this city;   235
For whom, and not for Tybalt, Juliet pined.
You, to remove that siege of grief from her,
Betrothed and would have married her perforce
To County Paris. Then comes she to me
And with wild looks bid me devise some mean   240
To rid her from this second marriage,
Or in my cell there would she kill herself.
Then gave I her (so tutored by my art)
A sleeping potion; which so took effect
As I intended, for it wrought on her   245
The form of death. Meantime I writ to Romeo
That he should hither come as° this dire night
To help to take her from her borrowed grave,
Being the time the potion's force should cease.
But he which bore my letter, Friar John,   250
Was stayed by accident, and yesternight
Returned my letter back. Then all alone
At the prefixèd hour of her waking
Came I to take her from her kindred's vault,
Meaning to keep her closely at my cell   255
Till I conveniently could send to Romeo.
But when I came, some minute ere the time
Of her awakening, here untimely lay
The noble Paris and true Romeo dead.

---

229. date of breath: remaining period of life.
247. as: on.

She wakes; and I entreated her come forth   260
And bear this work of heaven with patience;
But then a noise did scare me from the tomb,
And she, too desperate, would not go with me,
But, as it seems, did violence on herself.
All this I know, and to the marriage   265
Her nurse is privy;° and if aught in this
Miscarried by my fault, let my old life
Be sacrificed some hour before his time
Unto the rigor of severest law.

Prince.

We still° have known thee for a holy man.   270
Where's Romeo's man? What can he say to this?

Balthasar.

I brought my master news of Juliet's death;
And then in post he came from Mantua
To this same place, to this same monument.
This letter he early bid me give his father,   275
And threat'ned me with death, going in the vault,
If I departed not and left him there.

Prince.

Give me the letter. I will look on it.
Where is the county's page that raised the watch?
Sirrah, what made your master in this place?   280

Boy.

He came with flowers to strew his lady's grave;
And bid me stand aloof, and so I did.
Anon comes one with light to ope the tomb;
And by and by my master drew on him;
And then I ran away to call the watch.   285

Prince.

This letter doth make good the friar's words,
Their course of love, the tidings of her death;
And here he writes that he did buy a poison

265–266. **to the marriage . . . privy:** The nurse knows about the marriage.
270. **still:** always.

Of a poor pothecary and therewithal
Came to this vault to die and lie with Juliet.   290
Where be these enemies? Capulet, Montague,
See what a scourge is laid upon your hate,
That heaven finds means to kill your joys with love,
And I, for winking at° your discords too,
Have lost a brace° of kinsmen. All are punished.   295

Capulet.
O brother Montague, give me thy hand.
This is my daughter's jointure,° for no more
Can I demand.

Montague.   But I can give thee more;
For I will raise her statue in pure gold,
That whiles Verona by that name is known,   300
There shall no figure at such rate° be set
As that of true and faithful Juliet.

Capulet.
As rich shall Romeo's by his lady's lie—
Poor sacrifices of our enmity!

Prince.
A glooming peace this morning with it brings.   305
    The sun for sorrow will not show his head.
Go hence, to have more talk of these sad things;
    Some shall be pardoned, and some punishèd;
For never was a story of more woe
Than this of Juliet and her Romeo.   [*Exeunt omnes.*]   310

---

294. winking at: shutting his eyes at (in other words, "ignoring").
295. brace: pair (Mercutio and Paris).
297. jointure: property passed on to a woman after her husband's death.
301. rate: value.

A Commentary

Shakespeare in the Video Store

Film and television have brought Shakespeare's plays to millions of viewers and confirmed the playwright's position as a world treasure. *Hamlet* has been by far the most popular of his plays, with forty-seven film versions of all or part of the tragedy (as of 1994). The earliest *Hamlet* movie was made in Paris in 1900. This black-and-white silent film had an interesting reversal of the custom of Shakespeare's time, in which boys took women's roles onstage: The role of Hamlet was played by the great Sarah Bernhardt (1844–1923).

For almost a century, film productions of Shakespeare have showcased some of our most distinguished actors: Laurence Olivier, Vanessa Redgrave, Richard Burton, John Gielgud, Katharine Hepburn, Mel Gibson, Glenn Close, Denzel Washington. Between 1978 and 1985, a partnership between the British Broadcasting Corporation (BBC) and Time Warner, Inc., completed the ambitious project of filming all of Shakespeare's plays for television. Now Shakespeare is accessible as never before: A performance of one of his plays is as near as your local video store.

But critics have pointed out drawbacks in the performance of these plays on screen. For example, they argue that film controls our perceptions of the plays and deprives us of the tension we feel when seeing the plays live, in the theater. Film and television productions of Shakespearean comedy are at another disadvantage, since the actors can't respond to the feedback of a live audience. Such feedback is unpredictable, but actors say it's critical in comedy.

Not every Shakespeare movie has had celebrity performers. An outstanding example of a director's success with young unknown actors is Franco Zeffirelli's film *Romeo and Juliet* (1968). A comparison between the film script and the play's text shows the great extent to which the camera does in film what dialogue does onstage: Zeffirelli retained only about a third of Shakespeare's lines. He made other changes as well. Some lines are rearranged within scenes, and a few episodes—for example, the apothecary scene and the death of Paris—are dropped altogether.

The changes in the text of *Romeo and Juliet* are controversial, but most critics have agreed that the fiery, youthful passion of Zeffirelli's film faithfully catches the spirit of Shakespeare's play. The film is stunningly beautiful, in part because of the attractive young actors—Leonard Whiting as Romeo and Olivia Hussey as Juliet—and in part because of the dark beauty of the Italian hill towns Zeffirelli used as a setting for the tragedy. Three decades later, Zeffirelli's film is widely acknowledged to represent Shakespeare on screen at its best.

A Commentary

No Actresses and No R-Rated Love Scenes

On a visit to Venice in 1608, the English traveler Thomas Coryate recorded his astonishment: "For I saw women act, a thing I never saw before, though I have heard that it hath been sometimes used in London." Coryate was surprised because at the time, in London, boy actors between the ages of about ten and eighteen regularly took the parts of women onstage.

The roots of this custom were bound up with the origins of medieval drama. Centuries earlier, in English cathedrals, stories from the Bible were acted in brief plays. The performers—all male—came from the clergy, and they were assisted by choirboys. It wasn't until 1660 that women were permitted on the English stage—by the express order of King Charles II, whose fondness for the theater (and actresses) was to become a mark of his reign.

Boy actors were divided into two categories. There were members of all-boy companies, like the Children of St. Paul's Cathedral and the Children of the Chapel Royal. These young players enjoyed such popularity (and made so much money for their business managers) that star actors were in great demand. From the records of a 1602 legal case, we know that one schoolboy named Thomas Clifton was actually kidnapped and forced to join the Chapel Children. His father had to sue to get him back.

Other boy actors were apprentices to individual actors in the adult companies. These boys were preparing for a professional career. They took women's parts onstage for several years before and during adolescence. (It was one of these boy actors who took the part of Juliet.) When they were in their late teens, they switched to men's roles.

Some evidence suggests that Elizabethan actors trained their voices to be higher pitched, for both speaking and singing—so the difference between boys' voices and those of adults might have been less noticeable in Shakespeare's time. In any case, for a part such as Juliet—who is not yet fourteen when she makes her first appearance—costume and makeup for a boy actor could have easily sustained the illusion. Unlike actors and actresses in movies today, the young lovers in Shakespeare's play would have avoided physical contact. The words suggested the intensity of their feelings.

Casting boys as women on the Shakespearean stage had another unexpected twist. Plays with heroines in male disguise were highly popular at the time. Shakespeare wrote five such dramas, including *The Merchant of Venice, As You Like It,* and *Twelfth Night.* In these cases, boys played women who disguised themselves as young men. The mind boggles at the layers of illusion.

A Letter

"My Very Dear Sarah"
by Major Sullivan Ballou

During the American Civil War, 4,500 men were killed, wounded, or captured in a battle in Virginia called Bull Run by the North and Manassas by the South. A week before the battle, an officer in the Union Army, Major Sullivan Ballou, wrote a love letter to his wife, Sarah, who was in Rhode Island.

July 14, 1861
Camp Clark, Washington

My very dear Sarah:

The indications are very strong that we shall move in a few days—perhaps tomorrow. Lest I should not be able to write again, I feel impelled to write a few lines that may fall under your eye when I shall be no more. . . .

I have no misgivings about, or lack of confidence in the cause in which I am engaged, and my courage does not halt or falter. I know how strongly American Civilization now leans on the triumph of the Government, and how great a debt we owe to those who went before us through the blood and sufferings of the Revolution. And I am willing—perfectly willing—to lay down all my joys in this life to help maintain this Government and to pay that debt. . . .

Sarah my love for you is deathless, it seems to bind me with mighty cables that nothing but Omnipotence could break; and yet my love of Country comes over me like a strong wind and bears me unresistibly on with all these chains to the battle field.

The memories of the blissful moments I have spent with you come creeping over me, and I feel most gratified to God and to you that I have enjoyed them so long. And hard it is for me to give them up and burn to ashes the hopes of future years, when, God willing, we might still have lived and loved to-gether, and seen our sons grown up to honorable manhood, around us. I have, I know, but few and small claims upon Divine Providence, but something whispers to me—perhaps it is the wafted prayer of my little Edgar, that I shall return to my loved ones unharmed. If I do not my dear Sarah, never forget how much I love you, and when my last breath escapes me on the battle field, it will whisper your name. Forgive my many faults and the many pains I have caused you. How thoughtless and foolish I have often times been! How gladly would I wash out with my tears every little spot upon your happiness. . . .

But, O Sarah! if the dead can come back to this earth and flit unseen around those they loved, I shall always be near you; in the gladdest days and in the darkest nights . . . <u>always</u>, <u>always</u>, and if there be a soft breeze upon your cheek, it shall be my breath, as the cool air fans your throbbing temple, it shall be my spirit passing by. Sarah do not mourn me dead; think I am gone and wait for thee, for we shall meet again. . . .

Major Ballou was killed in the first battle of Bull Run, a week after he wrote this letter.

An Editorial

Romeo and Juliet in Bosnia
by Bob Herbert

The potential for clashes among the numerous ethnic groups in Eastern Europe goes back hundreds of years. Ethnic resentments in present-day Bosnia (formerly part of Yugoslavia), which simmered through foreign invasions and two world wars, were held in check by years of Communist rule. After communism collapsed in Yugoslavia in early 1990, civil war, and all its tragic consequences, erupted.

One of the many divisions in Bosnia is that between the Eastern Orthodox Serbs and the Muslims. Hatred and intolerance between these two religious groups ended the lives of a young couple in the capital city of Sarajevo (sä'rä'ye·vô). Their story prompted this editorial, written in 1994, when the civil war in Bosnia was at its height.

If you watch *Frontline* Tuesday night on PBS, you will see the story of two ordinary young people, Bosko Brkic, an Eastern Orthodox Serb, and Admira Ismic, a Muslim, who met at a New Year's Eve party in the mid-1980s, fell in love, tried to pursue the most conventional of dreams, and died together on a hellish bridge in Sarajevo.

The documentary, called "Romeo and Juliet in Sarajevo," achieves its power by focusing our attention on the thoroughly human individuals caught up in a horror that, from afar, can seem abstract and almost unimaginable. It's one thing to hear about the carnage caused by incessant[1] sniper fire and the steady rain of mortar shells on a city; it's something quite different to actually witness a parent desperately groping for meaning while reminiscing about a lost daughter.

For viewers overwhelmed and desensitized by the relentless reports of mass killings and mass rapes, the shock of "Romeo and Juliet in Sarajevo" is that what we see is so real and utterly familiar. We become riveted by the mundane. Bosko and Admira could be a young couple from anywhere, from Queens, or Tokyo, or Barcelona.

We learn that they graduated from high school in June of 1986 and that both were crazy about movies and music. Admira had a cat named Yellow that she loved, and Bosko liked to play practical jokes.

Admira's father, Zijo, speaking amid clouds of cigarette smoke, says, "Well, I knew from the first day about that relationship and I didn't have anything against it. I thought it was good because her guy was so likable, and after a time I started to love him and didn't regard him any differently than Admira."

Admira's grandmother, Sadika Ismic, was not so sanguine. "Yes, I did have something against it," she says. "I thought, 'He is Serb, she is a Muslim, and how will it work?'"

For Admira and Bosko, of course, love was the answer to everything. While Bosko was away on compulsory military service soon after high school, Admira wrote: "My dear love, Sarajevo at night is the most beautiful thing in the world. I guess I could live somewhere else but only if I must or if I am forced. Just a little beat of time is left until we are together. After that, absolutely nothing can separate us."

---

1. **incessant** (in·ses'ənt): never ceasing.

Sarajevo at the time was a cosmopolitan city coming off the triumph of the 1984 Winter Olympics. With a population of Serbs, Croats, Muslims, Jews, and others, the city had become a symbol of ethnic and religious tolerance, a place where people were making a serious attempt to live together in peace.

But civilization is an exceedingly fragile enterprise, and it's especially vulnerable to the primal madness of ethnic and religious hatreds. Simple tolerance is nothing in the face of the relentless, pathetic, and near-universal need to bolster the esteem of the individual and the group by eradicating the rights, and even the existence, of others.

When the madness descended on Sarajevo, Bosko Brkic faced a cruel dilemma. He could not kill Serbs. And he could not go up into the hills and fire back down on his girlfriend's people. Says his mother, Rada: "He was simply a kid who was not for the war."

Bosko and Admira decided to flee Sarajevo. To escape, they had to cross a bridge over the Miljacka River in a no man's land between the Serb and Muslim lines. Snipers from both sides overlooked the bridge.

It has not been determined who shot the lovers. They were about two thirds of the way across the bridge when the gunfire erupted. Both sides blame the other. Witnesses said Bosko died instantly. Admira crawled to him. She died a few minutes later. The area in which they were shot was so dangerous that the bodies remained on the bridge, entwined, for six days before being removed.

Only the times and places change. Bosnia today, Rwanda and Burundi tomorrow. Jews versus Arabs, Chinese versus Japanese, blacks versus whites. There are various ostensible reasons for the endless conflicts—ideological differences, border disputes, oil—but dig just a little and you will uncover the ruinous ethnic or religious origins of the clash.

The world stands helpless and sometimes depressed before the madness. Millions upon millions dead, millions more to die. It is not just the curse of our times. It seems to be the curse of all time.

—from *The New York Times*
May 8, 1994

A News Feature

Dear Juliet
by Lisa Bannon

Any man that can write may answer a letter.
—William Shakespeare
Romeo and Juliet, Act II, Scene 4

VERONA, Italy—Fate bequeathed a strange legacy to this small city in northern Italy.

As the setting for Shakespeare's sixteenth-century tragedy *Romeo and Juliet,* Verona inherited the curiosity of literary scholars, a celebrated theatrical tradition, and several hundred thousand tourists a year.

In the bargain, the city also became the star-crossed lovers' capital of the world.

"We don't know how it started exactly," explains Giulio Tamassia, the bespectacled city spokesman for matters relating to Romeo and Juliet. "But one day in the thirties, these letters started arriving unprompted—addressed to Juliet. At a certain point somebody decided Juliet should write back."

Juliet's Address
What began sixty years ago as an occasional correspondence has grown into an industry. This year more than one thousand letters from the lovelorn will arrive in Verona, addressed to Shakespeare's tragic heroine. Many of them land on Mr. Tamassia's desk, with no more address than: Juliet, Italy.

"They tend to be sentimental," says Mr. Tamassia, rifling through stacks of musty airmail in the cramped studio that serves as Juliet's headquarters. Inside big pink folders are thousands of sorrowful letters, break-your-heart tales of love and loss. They come from all over—a teenage girl in Guatemala, a businessman in Boston, a high school teacher in London. Some but not many are written by students in Shakespearean language. About two percent of letters received are addressed to Romeo, but Juliet replies.

"Writing the letter itself is really the first step toward solving the problem," says Mr. Tamassia, a fifty-nine-year-old retired businessman who wants it known at the outset that he himself is not Juliet. He is more her correspondence secretary.

"People express feelings in the letters that they would never admit to the person they love. Juliet's story inspires them," he says.

A Saudi Version

After much rummaging, he pulls out one of his favorites—describing a modern equivalent of the Montague-Capulet family rivalry.

Hala, an eighteen-year-old Saudi Arabian, wrote in March that she had fallen in love with the only son of her family's mortal enemy. Years ago, in Pakistan, her great-grandfather was responsible for the execution of a man who was using his property for smuggling heroin. From that time on, war was declared between the two families.

Now Hala was in love with a descendant of the executed man. "I am torn between the love for my family, which has made me what I am today, and my love for Omer, the man of my dreams," she wrote.

"Please reply quickly . . . my love, my life and future all depend on your answer."

—from *The Wall Street Journal*